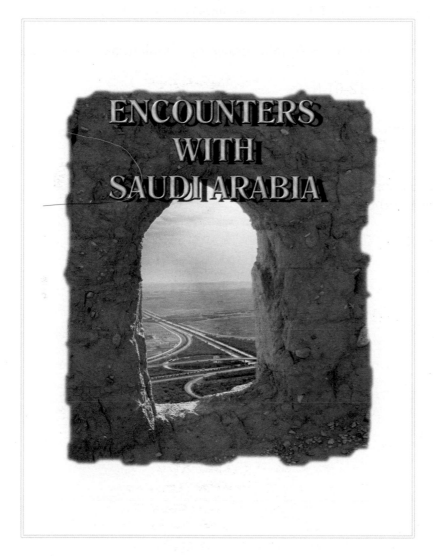

ENCOUNTERS WITH SAUDI ARABIA

Edited by:
Abdullmohsin H. Mosallam

Ministry of Information

© Ministry of Information, 1999
King Fahd National Library Cataloging-in- Publication Data

Encounters with Saudi Arabia \ Edited by Abdullmohsin H. Mosallam - Riyadh
296 p, 19x23 cm.
ISBN: 9960-612-01-5
1- Saudi Arabia History   2- Saudi Arabia Travels and
I-Mosallam, Abdullmohsin (cd)

915.31 dc   4050/19
Legal Deposit no. 4050/19
ISBN: 9960-612-01-5

KINGDOM OF
SAUDI ARABIA

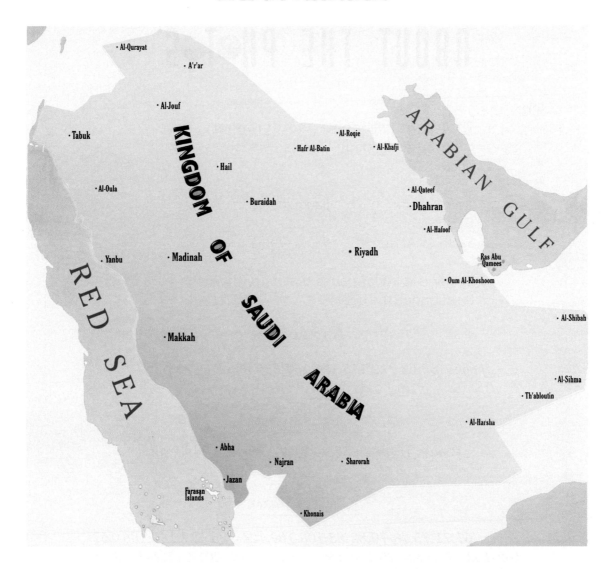

Population: 17,985,000
Density: 8.03/km2
Urban: 77%
Capital: Riyadh, 1,250,000
Life expectancy : 71 female, 68 male

Area : 2,239,690 km2
Highest point : Al-Sawda Mt. (Abha) , 3,207 m
Lowest point : Sea level
GDP : $128,840,000,000
Per capita: $7,158

ABOUT THE PHOTOS

Three professional photographers have contributed through their camera lenses to this book:

Ayed Al-Turky   Saudi Arabia
Garth Hyland   Australia
Saleh Al-Azzaz   Saudi Arabia

Below is a list of pages that carry their photos throughout the book:

AYED AL-TURKY

Pages: 35,62,110,115,196-197,234-235,241,258-259 .

GARTH HYLAND

Pages: 41,48-49,57,90-91,97,104,213,249,226.

SALEH AL-AZZAZ

Pages: 67,71,75,78-79,82-83,108-109,124-125,127,147,156-157 162-163,173,178-179,184-185,189,192 ,200-201-217,248 , 252-253,263,268-269,270,272-273,281,284-285.

CONTENTS

INTRODUCTION

In a fast-moving world, where religion is often subordinated to material considerations or relegated entirely to a small, quiet corner in a busy life, the *muezzin*'s call to prayer five times each day can come as a surprise to the visitor to the Kingdom of Saudi Arabia. The steadfast faith of Saudis as they turn towards the Holy City of Makkah and kneel in prayer has made an impact on the minds of many visitors, leading them to question and reassess the diverse and often conflicting influences that impinge on modern life.

This book attempts to capture the impact of the Kingdom on a number of its visitors. Here you will find the accounts of the businessman and the casual visitor, of men and women, the old and not so old. They recount in their own words their encounters in the Kingdom–the place, the people, how the people relate to each other and, of course, to their religion, Islam.

It is perhaps important to make clear what this book is not. It is not a research study on Saudi Arabia. Books of every kind have been published about Saudi Arabia–coffee table portfolios, well-researched reference books; books full of facts and figures; authoritative accounts of the land, its history and its political, economic and social development.

Encounters with Saudi Arabia is a book that tell a different story. It is not the work of professional journalists or established writers. Here you will find no journalistic pre-conceptions, no crude stereotypes. Rather it is the honest response to the Kingdom by a number of individuals who have experienced Saudi Arabia first hand–who have, with open eyes and open minds, attempted to grasp the vastness of the country and its unique geography, the colourful waters of the Red Sea, the tranquility of the Najd desert, the cool invigorating air of the Asir Mountains and the hustle and bustle of its thriving and expanding metropolitan districts. All is here, faithfully set down, the pleasant surprises, the occasional disappointment, the repudiations of stereotypes, the rich tapestry of life as it is in the Kingdom.

It is my sincere wish that this book will paint a picture of the Kingdom as it really is–a country that is peaceful, safe and welcoming.

May I also extend my thanks to all those who, in any way, helped to make this project a reality.

Dr. Fuad Bin A. Al-Farsi
Minister Of Information

WIGGLE THE GLASS

BY: KEN FERGUSON

When I was six years old, my sister who was three, and I were the only children living at the US Consulate in Dhahran. The consulate was situated in the middle of the desert about half way between the Aramco camp and the airport. It occupied about one square kilometre of stony, blank desert surrounded by a sandstone wall. The same sandstone was used to construct some of the major buildings and residences inside.

Climbing on top of sand that had blown against the inner side of the wall I could peer over and watch the occasional herdsman following his goats and sheep. They were always singing songs to themselves. I would sit on the wall and watch the airplanes take off and land at the airport. They would drone slowly away, four propellers biting into the hot air, gradually gaining altitude. When they were landing I could see them lower their wheels, their tired engines rumbling and spluttering, dragging streams of black exhaust,in the late afternoon. Sometimes I would walk down to the stone row house in the corner of the compound and visit the off-duty Marines and play with their dog. Other times I would knock on the door of the interpreter knowing that he would always invite me in.

His name was Mahmoud Yousef and he was from Egypt. He was a short, round man with smooth brown skin. He wore silver wire-frame glasses and had a little goatee. When I knocked on his door he greeted me with a laugh and always acted as though he was pleasantly surprised. Sometimes, after letting me into his small apartment, he would sit back down and resume his writing of documents in Arabic that he was translating. I was only 10, and with some difficulty learning how to read and write English so it was all the same to me. He would teach me how to say "good morning", or "thank you".

"Mom, the way you say good morning is "Sparkle K".

Well, that's not too far off from "*Sabah Al-Khair.*" Mahmoud Yousef tolerated my visits and was always ready to teach me a new Arabic word. I even learned how to write my name in Arabic.

One day, my father announced at the dinner table that Mahmoud Yousef had invited me to accompany him on a trip to meet Emir Bin Jiluwi who lived in Dammam, a fishing village a short way up the coast from Al-Khobar. Sometimes we would drive to Dammam on Thursdays to buy large palm frond basketsful of jumbo shrimp that would stink up the house all afternoon as my parents boiled and cleaned them. The shrimp would then appear for days as unpleasant choking surprises in thick yellow curries, or as short pink grubs under cold, red cocktail sauce, or as nuggets of parental pleasure fried in batter.

"Do you know why Mahmoud Yousef wants you to go with him? You must have impressed him during your visits. He wants to share something special with you. You're lucky to meet the Emir. He is a famous and powerful man. When you shake his hand be sure that your grip is firm and that you look him straight in the *eyes*. You will behave yourself, not interrupt, and sit quietly. And remember to take off your shoes. Now I want you to learn how to say hello properly, and how to say thank you."

So I practiced, what I had already learned from Mahmoud Yousef, "*Salaam aleikum, salaam aleikum, salaam aleikum.* " And the reply: "*Aleikum as salaam. Ashkuraq ashkuraq.* "

"But Dad, Mahmoud Yousef said thank you is "*shukran*."

"Never mind, he said it was "Sparkle K" too didn't he?"

The next morning, about 9 O'clock before it became too hot, we drove to Dammam. I was dressed all in white like a miniature Foreign Service officer. White socks, white shoes, white shorts, white short sleeved shirt and a white belt. For some reason the diplomats dressed like hospital orderlies in those days. "We dress in white because it's cooler." "Then why am I still hot?" "Because you're not used to it."

In Dammam, the Emir lived in a white palace. On an island across the harbour from the palace were the ruins of a Portuguese fort. Sailing vessels lie on their sides in the mud. The roads were all dirt. Through the car window I could see boys my age running after hoops that they propelled and balanced with sticks. They held their robes up above their knees so that they could run faster. The driver parked the car in front of the palace and Mahmoud Yousef and I went up the stairs to be greeted by a servant at the doorway who stood by a collection of sandals and shoes. We added ours and then followed him down the hallway to the *majlis* (meeting hall). It was a dark and cool meeting room with high ceilings, thick carpets and cushions arranged in a rectangle before a low chair. More low, cushioned chairs were arranged against the walls, all around the room. The tall windows were open and the ceiling fans turned slowly. The humid air was cool and carried a light aroma of spoiled shrimp.

Emir Bin Jiluwi rose from his desk by a window and greeted Mahmoud Yousef with soft words and a kiss on both cheeks. The great man turned to me. He was very tall, and his face was darker than other Saudis. He was dressed in white robes and wore a light brown cloak with golden trim. He did not smile. He was, I learned later, one of King Abdul Aziz's loyal captains who had long ago helped the King to unify the country.

"Salaam aleikum", I said, standing at attention in my white diplomatic socks, gripping the tips of his four fingers as firmly as possible and looking up straight into his *eyes.*

"Wa aleikum as salaam", he said to me in a deep gentle voice. He went to a table and picked up a tin of boiled sweets which he offered to me. Perfectly sticky green, red and yellow balls wrapped in cellophane. I took a red one and he suggested that I take more.
I took three more red ones, looking to Mahmoud Yousef for approval. He looked away, smiling. The Emir gestured to the cushions as he sat on his low

"I had never drunk tea before. This was something not to tell my mother. I waited and watched. When Mahmoud Yousef took his first little sip, then I did. It was deliciously sweet. Ah, it was wonderful!"

chair sighing softly. He and Mahmoud Yousef then began to talk and the interpreter took out papers from his valise. I sat on my cushion, cross-legged, sucking on the red ball, focused on its cherry flavor, oblivious to all but the candy. I counted the three candy balls in my hand and considered the advantages of consuming them one at a time or all together. A rustling sound and the clinking of glass caused me to turn and see beside me the servant who had greeted us at the door. Now he leaned towards me holding a tray of tea glasses. They were miniature mugs with handles. Each of the glasses was already full of clear, red gold tea.

"Be careful. Take the glass by its handle. It is

very hot. Let it cool before you drink, " said Mahmoud Yousef. The tea was very hot, even when I held the handle. I almost spilled it as I hurried to put it down on the rug. Suddenly I forgot the red candy. I had never drunk tea before. This was something not to tell my mother. I waited and watched. When Mahmoud Yousef took his first little sip, then I did. It was deliciously sweet. Ah, it was wonderful! I drank the contents of the glass quickly. It was like watery syrup. Almost immediately, the servant was beside me, pouring a stream of tea into the glass. It gurgled and bubbled and made a little cloud of steam, and looked beautifully golden. After it cooled I drank it down quickly, relishing its sweetness, and amazed that unlike a glass of Pepsi, it was immediately refilled. I never had to worry that it was only half full, or nearly empty. It would be surely refilled as soon as I put the empty glass down.

I had three more glasses. Then, at the end of the fifth glass, my revelry was interrupted by Mahmoud Yousef's gentle voice, "You've had enough. What would your mother say?" He resumed his discussion with the Emir. In a state of obedient disappointment I turned to the servant with my "thank you."

Swiftly and expertly, he poured a stream of golden red tea into my glass. He was a Tea Genie! I had another full glass, which I hid next behind one of my crossed knees and then tried to drink as quickly and quietly as possible. Again I turned to the servant, and shaking my head, said "*la, shukran*" (No thank you). The Genie smiled, and again a curving stream of tea left spout of the pot and filled my glass.

I heard the Emir chuckling and turned to see him speaking to Mahmoud Yousef, both of them looking at me. " But please, you must have seen that I tried to say no more?" I said. "When you want no more, then hold the empty glass by its handle and wiggle your wrist. If you just say no more, then you will certainly receive more. You must wiggle your wrist like this," Mahmoud Yousef demonstrated.

I slowly and reluctantly finished my seventh glass of tea, then turned to the servant and wiggled my glass. Alas, the spell was broken and he took my cup, placed it on the tray and then collected the Emir's and Mahmoud Yousef's glasses. The coffee then followed, but it was bitter and one sip would have been enough. I quickly swallowed the contents of the little cup, and wiggled it with a sense of relief. Mahmoud Yousef laughed. Soon after, the meeting ended and I thanked the Emir, "*Shukran*" and bid him good-bye, "*Ma salaama*" and firmly shook his fingers, looking him straight in the eye. He smiled.

On the drive home, Mahmoud Yousef was worried what my mother would say if she knew that I'd had seven cups of tea. "Don't worry, Mahmoud. I won't tell. Will you?"

"No, I won't tell either," and he and the driver laughed.

"Thank you Mahmoud Yousef for taking me to meet the Emir today. I want to pay you back."

"Oh no, my friend, you cannot do that. You must pay it forward. You have time to learn what I mean."

A few months later, when the cold season had begun, my father came home and said that he and I had been invited to join a hunting party. We would hunt the *habara* (bustard) bird with *saqr* (falcons). Important people from the consulate and Aramco were to travel to Al-Jubail which was many hours drive north. There, we would be guests of the Emir of Al-Jubail and his falconers. Again I received strict instructions on behaviour and etiquette.

I was put to bed early since we would have to get up early and then stay awake all that night. At three o'clock I was out of bed before my father could finish saying "get up". We dressed, ate a little breakfast and then drove with the other consulate staff to Aramco. We transferred from our town cars into big red Dodge sedans with white numbers painted on their roofs. They were special desert cars that sat high off the ground on fat black sand tyres. They had canvas water bags hung over their over-sized radiators and long whip antennas for their two-way radios. Their engines made powerful growls as they were revved by their drivers. There was a fuel truck and a water truck. There were me-

chanics and Bedouin guides. The long line of vehicles rolled through the main gate and turned north
on the road to Ras Tanura. About an hour later the
convoy left the paved road and followed a desert
track to Al-Jubail

At mid-dawn we arrived at the low, brown, mud
buildings of the Emir of Al-Jubail. We were all welcomed into his *majlis* . Maybe forty of us sat on cushions in a big rectangle. Several servants glided into
the room bearing trays full of tea glasses. Others followed them carrying big tea pots. Oh boy, tea!

My cup was filled with golden red tea. While I waited
for it to cool, I watched my father burn his mouth
and then put the glass down in a hurry, secretively
wincing and rubbing his hot fingers on his pants. In
a few minutes, I began to drink the delicious brew,
loving its sweetness. Then, all too soon, the little glass
was empty, but the Tea Genie filled it almost instantly.
A long steaming arc of tea curved through the cold
morning air and gurgled into my glass. So too was
my father's glass filled. He held up his glass with his
little finger sticking out and blew on it, just like the

other diplomats did, and then sipped, a little painfully. But my newly filled glass was poised on the rug before me, sharing my little space, awaiting my pleasure. It cooled, and I drank it slowly, and continuously, until it was almost gone. No worry, there was more. It was magic. Then I heard my father's voice.
"That's enough."
"Yes Dad."

Despondently I watched the Tea Genie approach staring fixedly at our empty glasses. My father held out his empty glass to the servant, said "No more, thank you" and then watched his glass being filled. He quickly placed it on the rug, rubbing his fingers.

"You have to wiggle the glass Dad, if you don't want anymore," I offered.
"Don't be silly."

"Okay Dad," I said as I obediently extended my glass to the servant and wiggled it. My father stared in disbelief as the Tea Genie took my glass and placed it with the other empty ones on his tray. Then, to my supreme pleasure, he turned toward me, and smiled as he drained his glass and happily wiggled it before the Tea Genie. I was immensely gratified. Thanks to my two wise Arab friends I had, for the first time in my life, taught my father a lesson, a rare pleasure even now, many years later.

It has taken me a long time to even begin to understand what "pay it forward" means. Even now, too many years later, I find new ways to interpret the request. Certainly Mahmoud Yousef would be proud to know that I seek and sometimes find a few who are capable of paying forward my offerings to them. He and the Emir would be happy to know that I still drink my tea as sweet as possible, and when I am with my Arab friends I am the last to wiggle the glass.

 Former Aramco employee

A Friend In Need

BY: DR. ROBERT PORTER

*I*t has not been difficult to re-call occasions when I have had pleasant encounters with Sau-dis over the past 14 years; in fact they are of frequent occurrence. I only have to open the hood of my car to have a passer-by–often a complete stranger–ask me if I need help. In a supermarket, a fellow shop-per will recommend certain goods or ask my advice on others. Unable to find my way around a new office block, I will soon be approached by a friendly person anxious to help. On the roads my experi-ences are mixed; polite Saudis will often make way to allow me to enter a line of traffic. These balance the negative experience with those drivers who double-park while they do some roadside shopping. But even the latter bear no ill-feeling when I call them from the shop to allow me to drive away; they will be very apologetic and disarm me with a cheer-ful "*ma'lish*". Strangely enough, one ends up with a smile instead of a scowl!

A particular occasion that remains in my mind is the time I locked myself and my wife out of our apartment. I have passed out of that door thousands of times and I ALWAYS have my key with me as I close the self-locking door but this was the exception that proves the rule. More-over, I did not realise what I had done until we returned to the apartment, after an overseas vacation, three weeks later at 3 am. How were we to get in? I had always regarded the apart-ment is virtually burglar-proof. The lock on the door is very strong. The windows and the ve-randah are 12 metres above the ground with only the smooth bare walls beneath them. I did not know what to do. I couldn't find a locksmith in the middle of the night and could not break the door down; I could not reach the windows or verandah and anyway the windows and the ve-randah doors were locked on the inside. But help came in the shape of my Saudi neighbour, Saleh, who happened to be returning from night-shift duties with his company. In fact, this was our first meeting with him because he had moved into his apartment when we had been away, but he was determined to help us. He was certain we could find a way in, and he was, indeed, the very spirit of optimism. He invited my wife to take tea with his wife while he and I sought access to my flat.

First he led me down to the basement where he found a ladder, but alas, it proved much too short for our purpose. Then he proposed to climb up the wall to the verandah. He is a young man and very agile, but I doubted his ability to scale a smooth wall. I had to dissuade him, reminding him of his wife and three small children, as a fall from the area of the verandah would almost certainly be fatal. So we returned to the floor where my flat was situated and we found that a window on the landing was opposite the bathroom window of my apartment. But between the two windows was a 12-metre drop to the basement. Apparently oblivious to danger, Saleh reached over the black void until his body was almost horizontal, and somehow he managed to haul himself across to the very narrow ledge outside our window. It was locked, but after a lot of vigorous shaking, which could easily have sent Saleh plummeting to the ground, he got the window open and disappeared inside the bathroom. In a trice he had the front door open and had reappeared on the landing.

Saleh had saved the day for us and we expressed our deep gratitude. A little later, as my wife and I were sitting in, we heard a tap on the door. We opened to find Saleh's small daughter standing there with a big bowl of fruit.

Dr. Robert Porter is British, he perviously worked as the Chairman of the Engineering Department, English Language Center, King Abdul Aziz University, Jeddah. Dr. Porter has been living in the Knigdom for 14 years.

Bedouin Little League

By: Larry Ives

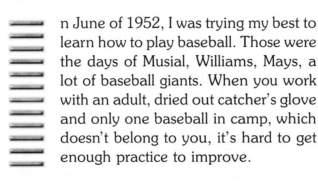

n June of 1952, I was trying my best to learn how to play baseball. Those were the days of Musial, Williams, Mays, a lot of baseball giants. When you work with an adult, dried out catcher's glove and only one baseball in camp, which doesn't belong to you, it's hard to get enough practice to improve.

My hometown at the time was Umni'neck, Saudi Arabia, located somewhat south of Abqaiq, past the Aindar plant. This is a pretty remote place on the great desert, not easy to get a baseball game going. But, by combining my Dad's dried out old catcher's mitt, and Teddy Eastwood's mangled baseball, we were playing the great American sport 10-thousand miles from our homeland.

Our little games were down from the portables close to the fence, and we started to get an audience of Bedouin children who sat on the dunes closest to the chain link fence. They and their families would come and go, sometimes none were around, and other times, there would be four or five tribes camped outside our fenced off camp.

For a few weeks all the tents camped around us disappeared. There was no one to watch our ball games, and the ball players dwindled away. It got down to just Teddy and I trying to catch and throw the ball. One day, we looked up and there was a large camel, standing close to the fence, ridden by a concerned looking gentleman carrying a beautiful flintlock rifle, goat skin water bags slung on each side of the camel and trailed by two boys about our age.

The Saudi father turned and said something to the boys, and turned his camel, and trotted quickly out of sight over the dunes. The boys sat on the sand and fixed their attention toward us. I wish I could say that we all then somehow bonded and we taught them baseball, and became immediate friends, but the truth was, we were soon trading insults, made better by the fact they didn't know what we were saying, and we didn't know what they were saying. That was when the rock fight started.

It was a beauty of a rock fight. They would come up to the line, chuck their rock, we would come up and chuck ours. We then all stood around and admired who had thrown the rock the farthest in the general direction of the other side over the chain link fence dividing us. We did this until dark, and then, to our respective portables and tents, knowing we would continue tomorrow.

The next evening, we had an audience on each side, all the kids on our side of the fence, and several on their side, including Saudi girls, whom we had never seen. We met our opponents at the fence, and Teddy and I started tossing the ball back and forth, and somehow it evolved into us tossing the ball over the fence to them, and then they tossed it back. Soon, we backed up and were really throwing the ball, and then scooping it up and throwing it back over.

It seemed to go on for hours, and I had a lot of fun, just throwing and catching a baseball. Finally, it started to get dark. The last time one of the Bedouin boys threw the ball back over the fence, we walked down to the fence and called them down to us at the fence. We dug out the sand at the bottom of the fence, and poked the ball through to them, and with hand gestures told them to keep it. Their eyes got real big, and they started to try and give us things they had upon them. Teddy and I turned and ran away. The next time we went down to that part of the fence, their tents were gone.

Hope that baseball was passed down to a grandson that made the Little League World Series from Saudi Arabia.

 Former Aramco employee

Managing And Learning From Changes

By: Latchmawattie Raghubhans

Our lives undergo changes constantly. As individuals, our values, ways of life, aims and objectives change as we grow older. During the winter of 1993, I grew a bit weary and tired of the long, cold and dark days in the UK more, so I felt I needed a change of environment. I then decided to scan through the *Radiography Journal* to check what jobs were available abroad. I found there were vacancies in the Far East, Middle East and North America. After about five weeks, I began to get positive responses to all my applications. I was now in a bit of a quandary being spoilt for choice. After some deliberation I decided that I would take up the offer that came first. This was from Saudi Arabia. Thus I immediately started preparations to take up this offer.

After resigning my post as a Senior Radiographer in UK I had exactly one and a half months to make all the necessary arrangements to wind down my activities there before I rushed off to the sun, sand and sea. I had a frantic, hectic six weeks to sort my affairs out, but I managed. I was able to travel to Saudi Arabia as scheduled.

Upon arrival in Saudi Arabia, I was faced with a culture shock. By this I mean removal or distortion of many of the familiar things I encountered at home and the substitution for them with other ways, which I found strange and different. I clearly underwent four stages of culture shock, which are as follows:

Stage one–My incubation period. In this stage I found the Saudi culture intriguing. The hosts (Saudis) were very courteous and my expectations for the future were positive. The period of fascination and adventure was primary and lasted for roughly six weeks.

Stage two–The crisis period. It was the period when I began to encounter genuine difficulties. The activities of daily living that had previously been taken for granted became grave (insurmountable). I found the heat oppressive and intolerable. I was mentally and physically fatigued. I became bored, lacked intellectual stimulation and found work tedious. I required solitude, began to read more and listen to the wireless in my spare time. Fortunately I was able to recover from this stage within two months. Quick enough not to hamper my job performance and morale.

Stage three–After my recuperation, I began to understand some of the ways of the Saudi culture. I also began to regain my sense of humour and develop self-awareness. I started to make adjustments in my habits so as to gradually ease myself into my work and home environment in the third and fourth months of my stay.

Stage four–The post recovery period (After six months). Now I was fully acclimatised and I accepted the host culture. By this time I really began to enjoy my job and my Saudi experiences.

I began to ask questions to become more comfortable. I made friends with my colleagues and

> "Upon arrival in Saudi Arabia, I was faced with a culture shock. By this I mean removal or distortion of many of the familiar things I encountered at home and the substitution for them with other ways, which I found strange and different."

understood them more. I tried very hard not to get hung up on negativism. I made an effort not to isolate myself, so I mixed with other nationalities. I participated in recreational activities. I also enrolled myself for a course in Arabic. I managed to successfully complete Level 1 in Arabic. This course enabled me to ease the communication barrier, which was one of the main reasons for my culture shock.

To adjust more, I summoned my own personal strengths and support during my periods of difficulty. I also used my spirit of self-awareness and adaptability to overcome my difficulties. On hindsight, I was able to succeed because I could perceive my problems, analyse them and then generate ideas on how to solve them.

When I look back, I give myself a pat on the shoul-

der. I feel quite satisfied at having adjusted so well in my job and home environments. Had I remained in UK I would never have had such a wonderful opportunity of working with so many different nationalities as a team, all under the same roof.

Working in a hospital environment, all professional disciplines form a continuous link in the chain system to provide a service to the patient. I can indeed say this system is well co-ordinated and integrated. It has been a great opportunity for me to see how work is performed by different nationalities especially when we work and live in a community atmosphere.

I am really amazed to see how the desert and difficult terrain has been transformed into prolific vegetation and scenic beauty. The Kingdom continues to invest heavily in its infrastructure and massive strategic programmes are being developed for the benefit of the Saudi population.

 Latchmawattie Raghubhans is a British national. He is a Radiotherapy Technician at King Abdul Aziz Hospital, Jeddah, and has been living in the Kingdom for four and-a-half years.

Jabrin And Al–Kuhn Expedition

BY: CHARLES ARMSTRONG

0400 hours, Thursday, November 25, 1993: Final loading of the Blazer and recheck of the "to take" list. Brent and I are heading out on a desert expedition at 0600 and everything must be right. The plan is to meet Salim Abukhamsin and his nephew at 0615 at the drilling tool house to begin a trip south to the ancient village of Jabrin. The name of this village has four correct pronunciations: Jabrin, Jabreen, Yabrin, and Yabreen.

The village is some 100 kilometres south of Haradh, Saudi Arabia. It's also some 100 kilometres south of the southernmost paved road in the Eastern Province of Saudi Arabia.

We would drive across the desert on or near "skid" roads, "Bedouin" trails or nothing. Lots of nothing. Moonscape barren. Only the occasional salt bush and the occasional abandoned vehicle that died en route were evident. We were a group of five men and five boys. Eight Saudis and two Americans. We were travelling in four vehicles; two new Toyota Land Cruisers and two vintage Chevy Blazers. Salim and his nephew, Ahmad, were in one Blazer and Brent and I were in the other, older one. Qurian Al Hajri, of Bedouin descent and master desert reconnoitre, with his two sons, Mohammad and Jassar, were in the newest Land Cruiser. Jawad, Riyadh, and his son, Omar, filled out the party.

The meeting at the tool house, was right on time. Salim and I briefly discussed the driving plan, then headed out. I figured it would take 45 minutes to complete "leg one" of the trip. That was Dhahran to Abqaiq. "Leg two": Abqaiq to the police station at Udailiyah would take one hour. Exactly right. We were to meet Qurian there at 0800. That, we did.

At about 0830, after we had all greeted each other and told a few stories, we started "Leg

three" which was the 117 kilometers to Haradh. The plan was to fuel up (gasoline and snacks at the last gas station/grocery store) then proceed south across country. Interesting but there were 10 other vehicles at the Haradh gas station when we got there. All crazy Americans out to explore the real desert! We left Haradh station at 1000 hours and headed toward Jabrin.

The desert south of Haradh immediately becomes
desolate. There are very few plants and no signs of
human activity except for tire tracks and an occasional muffler or discarded, blown tyre. I found that
Saudi "four-wheeling" isn't as it's done in the States.
Here, it's "pedal to the metal" driving. I was minorly
uptight for the first 30 or so kilometres. I knew I was
just about to hit a "whoop-de-do" at any minute and
have my load of groceries, bedrolls, cots, lanterns,
etc. come flying forward onto my head. No problem
though.

Qurian, the leader, knew what he was doing and how
fast we could safely go. When the "skid" road was
smooth (which was rarely), we'd drive on it. Otherwise, we drove across barren desert, spaced such that
the dust from one vehicle would not obscure the vision (or stick to the teeth) of other drivers.

After an hour or so of desert driving, we stopped for
a very necessary "lizard bleeding" break and let the
kids kick a soccer ball for a bit. During this stop, Brent

collected some very interesting rocks that looked like petrified brain coral. We decided they were actually igneous rocks that had been eroded in a very strange fashion. After bleeding all lizards and kicking the soccer ball, we resumed the wild, cross country ride. After a relatively short time, several hills loomed on the horizon. I told Brent that I guessed they were the destination. They are all very plateau-like in that they are flat on top. Flat except for the "pimples" that became evident as we got closer to them. These "pimples" are actually tumuli, or the graves of people who died and were buried there thousands of years ago. We drove up onto one of the hills and closely inspected several tumuli.

After the "tumuli tour", we headed down to the village of Jabrin proper. Remember, we are right in the middle of "nowhere". What are we greeted by as we enter the village? A large road sign proclaiming, "Welcome to Jabrin, the jewel of the desert". Jabrin is a very real little town with paved streets, gas stations, grocery stores, auto repair shops, electricity, running water and even satellite dishes for TV reception. We needed to buy some film and were told that it could be purchased up the street at the toy store. Sure enough, but the only problem was that the toy store was closed. The guy in the laundry next door, had the key and he opened up so we could get our film. Two rolls of 36 exposure each so Brent could shoot pictures freely.

The camp site: On the way, Riyadh and I got separated from Qurian and Salim. No problem. We found a huge pile of palm tree trunks that would make great firewood and decided to load them onto my Blazer while we waited to be re-united with the others. Brent got up on the roof of the Blazer and acted as catcher and organiser. We'd throw up a chunk of palm tree, he'd catch it, then organise it on the car top carrier. We finally camped at a location approximately 12 kilometres west of Jabrin. We camped where there was an abundance of burnable vegetation and clean, driveable sand.

Naturally, the first order of business was to establish a camp. Brent and I set out unloading

our Blazer and putting up our tent. The Saudi guys
got their tent up and got into some serious relaxation far faster than I did. They know how to do it
right. I fiddled around getting a stove, lantern, table,
cooking equipment, chairs, cots, traps, snake hood,
garbage bag, etc. organised. They got into story telling, date snacking and sleep 30 minutes before I was
done.

When the kids had their part of the work finished,
they set out placing traps to catch any of the unseen
desert denizens inhabiting the area. A preliminary
search indicated to me that there were numerous le-
gless lizards, mice and beetles in the area. Possibly
even sand boas. Signs of *jarboa'a* (desert rats) and
thub (lizard) were absent, though. It was these two
animals the kids had come equipped to catch. Omar
had a *jareed* (trap) that he was going to use to catch
a *thub*. He would simply find the lizard's den and
both entrance holes. His plan was to place the trap
over one hole then go around to the other one and
scare the animal out of the den into the trap.

The door would then be manually closed. Seemed
reasonable. No *thub* holes, though. Brent had three

"Have-a-heart" live catch traps for *jarboa'a*. He scouted the area during daylight hours for likely looking holes, then marked each of them with white flags on 36-inch brazing rod stakes. He then set the traps and baited them with gobs of peanut butter. All traps were to be checked periodically throughout the night.

We were to discover, much to our disappointment, that, due to the nearly full moon, there would be very little animal activity on the desert this night. Brent and I even went road hunting with powerful spotlights and, after an hour of searching, found nothing.

After setting up the camp, I started on the cooking part of next morning's breakfast. The same old "Armstrong camp food"- two pounds of hamburger, a bunch of potatoes, a bunch of onions, a bunch of bell peppers and a bunch of "Tony's" seasoning. Brown the hamburger, then add it and a little water, to the vegetables. Steam it for exactly that long then put it into the ice chest for next day's use. I was told the next morning that I'd overdone the *filfil* (pepper).

Along with a dozen hamburger patties, Qurian barbecued chicken and sheep and cooked a huge pot of rice. The rice was done on a small gas stove. Everything else was done on a very stout grill over an open fire. Not only is Qurian an absolute expert on the ways of the desert, he is also a master chef. The food he prepared was fit for royalty. Needless to say, there was a continuous supply of cardamom coffee and very hot, sweet tea.

An hour after dark, we all gathered on a long, narrow tarp and commenced to eat and eat until we were completely satiated. Then, some of us ate some more. Everybody went to sleep that night with a very full belly. *Al–Hamdulillah!* (thank God). Doing the dishes was easy. We simply laid out trays and pots in the desert for the creatures of the night to clean off uneaten food. Soap and water would come the next morning.

I stayed awake most of the night and was able to watch the setting of the moon and the progression of stars in their nightly march across the sky. The only sounds evident on this exceptionally still night were the low drone of the Jabrin village generators and a periodic grunt or snore from any of the group of deep sleepers in our camp. I was treated to a natural light show as meteor after meteor plummeted to earth in a blaze of glory. What a night! It was possibly the most beautiful night I'd experienced in many, many years. Dawn came much too soon.

As a pillar of sunlight was just starting to manifest itself skyward from the eastern horizon, Qurian and I started our respective breakfast chores. He got the fire going and I started to heat desert stew and coffee water. He brewed real coffee. One by one, bodies stirred. Singly and in trios, men and boys faced the west and performed sunrise prayers. There is something very poetic about prayers done in a natural setting. To me, it is so much more meaningful than praying in an artificial structure. To me, God and nature are very closely linked.

Shortly after the sun had fully cleared the eastern horizon, Qurian began cooking eggs. He boiled some and made a sort of scrambled omelet of the rest. Out came the cheese, the *khobous*, (bread) the sweet

" As a pillar of sunlight was just starting to manifest itself skyward from the eastern horizon, Qurian and me both started our respective break-fast chores. He got the fire going and I started to heat desert stew and coffee water. He brewed real coffee. One by one, bodies stirred.

crepes, the fruit, the coffee and the desert stew. Hungry men and boys again feasted. I was amazed! Even though my "stew" was greasy and over "filfiled" (spiced), it was con-sumed. No complaints. None that I heard anyway.

In that we wanted to be on the road by 1000 hours, camp break-ing began immediately after break-fast. The kids were directed by

48

Singly and in trios, men and boys faced the west and performed sunrise prayers. There is something very poetic about prayers done in a natural setting. To me, it is so much more meaningful than praying in an artificial structure. To me, God and nature are very closely linked ".

Salim to "police" the area and put anything non-biodegradable into black plastic trash bags. These, we carried to Jabrin for proper disposal. I was impressed. The only three items left behind were a gallon of kerosene and a camp chair—both for use by any Bedouin who wanted or needed them and a scattering of vegetable matter for the mice and birds.

The rough terrain had taken its toll on one of the vehicles, so our first stop would have to be in Jabrin to get an exhaust welded back on. While the work was being done, Qurian led us to an exquisite farm on the outskirts of the village. We entered through ornate steel doors into an absolute paradise. An outdoor *majlis* under an arbour and a permanent concrete floored tent were immediately evident. I was also amazed to see a California palm tree just inside the doors.

"The only sounds evident on this exceptionally still night were the low drone of the Jabrin village generators and a periodic grunt or snore from any of the group of deep sleepers in our camp."

The owner of this farm had a good touch for animal husbandry. He had erected a unique *hamam* (pigeon) coop on the roof of a two-storey utility building. The coop was built out of three-hole bricks and reminded me of a Dutch farm house. Random bricks had the holes pointing outward so the pigeons could come and go to and from the interior at will. Along the western margin of the compound were enclosures housing Asian wild turkey, quail, chickens and mallard ducks, Belgian flop-eared rabbits and geese. All were clean and healthy and had an over abundant supply of clean running water. In the centre of the compound, was a four-metre square wall enclosing a hand dug artesian well. The water was abundant and crystal clear.

With time running short, we rushed away from the farm, collected the now repaired and quiet vehicle, fuelled up (again gas and groceries) and headed out onto the desert. Our immediate destination was the village of Al-Khun which was some 79 kilometres to the north-east of Jabrin. One and a half hours later, we were amongst hundreds of the finest racing camels to be had, and the palatial mansions of their owners. Al- Khun, like Jabrin, is also in the "middle of nowhere". It was amazing to see huge, ultra-modern houses 80 kilometres from the nearest paved road.

Our route now was essentially due north to the Haradh farm project. It was an uneventful, high speed, rough drive of about one and a half hours. The Haradh farm project is a long, narrow band of ultra green alfalfa fields. The original plan was to install an aqueduct system of irrigation but this was obviously scrapped in favour of pivot systems. Hundreds and hundreds of defunct aqueduct sections lay scrapped on the side of the road. On the other side of the road, half circles of healthy alfalfa lay side by side for 30 kilometers. At the farm headquarters, thousands upon thousands of huge hay rolls were lying in covered storage, awaiting transport to places far to the north or west.

As we drove parallel to the farm project, I was fortunate to observe one falcon on the hunt. It was a male European kestrel. The migration had in fact, begun and I could now look forward to more sightings and possibly, a capture. A kestrel for Brent and a hur or female sharin for me.

We arrived back at the fuel station in Haradh at approximately 1245 hours and I put in SR18 worth of gas. Enough to get Brent and me all the way back to the house in Dhahran. Qurian, the generous gentleman that he is, immediately arranged a biriyani meal for all of us at a restaurant adjacent to the station. Brent and I reluctantly declined the invitation as my wife, Linda, said she wanted to prepare a traditional American "Thanksgiving" meal for us for Friday evening. We told her we would try to be home between 1600 and 1700 Friday evening. As it turned out, we backed into my driveway at exactly 1600 hours. Tired, beat, happy and healthy!

To me, life is what you've done. Not what you're going to do. I can't tell you factually about the good times I'm going to have, but I can sure expound on the good times I have had. Nobody can take memories away from me. Brent and I are very fortunate, indeed, to have had this experience. It is one he and I will remember fondly until our memories cease.

It is an experience like this that allows me to grow a little closer to my son and to see workmates in a different, more human light. Through experiences like this, my understanding and respect for these men grow. Understanding and respect will unite mankind. Brent and I are thankful that we had the opportunity to make this trip. We will do it again-but spend more time. We are also looking forward to the trip to the northern area next April or May.

 Former Aramco employee

THE TRAVELLER

BY: GORDON GOLDING

On a weekend trip, we were driving on a desert track in a remote area. As we drove through the sand and clumpy desert bushes or *dikaka*, there was nothing around us taller than 18 inches. It seemed impossible that anything larger than a rabbit could be there unseen.

From nowhere, a figure simply appeared at the side of the track. He was wearing the traditional flowing black robe. When the wind pushed it against him, it was obvious that he carried almost nothing on his person. He couldn't have had a canteen larger than a small flask. We stopped to talk to him.

I had heard of the Bedouin poets and the way they could create a poem as fast as one could simply speak, but I had never heard that Bedu poetry flowed like molten gold. When he said,

"Hello," he said it in poetry. Instead of "Peace be upon you", as I had always heard, he added a single word and it became rhyming, flowing poetry: *Salaamu Allah Alaikum*, or "May the peace of God be upon you". We listened intently to every word that came forth like a melody from him.

We gave him a ride and cold juice and did our best to make out his story. He had needed to go to a doctor. He had hitchhiked to the closest clinic and was now on the way back to where his tribe had been. But the pasture there had given out and his people had moved their flocks on. He had found himself in the middle of the desert, alone. The track we were on was seldom used. He had put his trust in Allah and had found a tiny patch of shade in which to wait, hoping for another traveller to happen along.

The depth of the dignity of the old Bedouin is hard for us Westerners to understand. When he saw us coming, he did not stand in the middle of the road and scream for help. He stood quiet and stately by the side of the road and gently asked for aid when we stopped. We might have driven past, but he trusted in Allah and the goodness of his fellow man.

"I had heard of the Bedouin poets
and the way they could create a poem
as fast as one could simply speak."

Sometime later, he asked to be dropped at the side of the track. We looked around. There was nothing all the way to the horizon. We offered to take him directly. He declined saying it was too close to bother and that the *dikaka* would be hard on the truck. We asked if he was sure that his people were close. He was sure he knew exactly where they would have moved on to. We gave him a last cup of tea and bid him farewell.

As he bid us farewell in return, he added one last thanks; "If you had not come, I surely would have died". There was no change in his composure; in that massive dignity that nothing in this world would shake. He stood and waved for a moment as we drove on.

Then he turned and set off across the trackless sand.

 Former Aramco employee

You Cannot Stay Away For Long

BY: CURTIS W. BRAND

y experience with the Kingdom of Saudi Arabia dates back to 1975, when Mobil Oil Corporation was still a shareholder of Aramco, and Saudi Arabia was poised for the phenomenal growth and development that was to change the Kingdom. My first job was linked to Aramco, which was already in transition in 1975. The Saudi Arabian government had acquired a 60 percent financial interest in Aramco and negotiations were soon to get underway between them and the Aramco shareholders to complete the total takeover of the company by the government. I assisted in these negotiations and feel that I was very much a part of history.

I stayed involved with Aramco until 1984 in various jobs for Mobil. During the late 1970's and early 1980's, Aramco experienced enormous growth in its business, very much like the rest of the Kingdom. They designed and built the Master Gas System that was to provide gas for the Kingdom's power generation, as well as serve as feedstock for the many petrochemical projects which have now been built as SABIC joint ventures in Jubail and Yanbu.

Aramco also significantly increased its crude production capabilities during this period. In many cases, the facilities built and operated by them were, and still are, the largest of their kind in the world. The company greatly expanded its Saudi workforce, providing training and jobs for thousands of young Saudis. During my involvement with them, when I was travelling between the US and Dhahran just about every month, I was privileged to get to know many young Saudi managers and professionals working for the company. I developed many friendships, which have lasted until today and I have seen a number of these Saudis go on to assume very senior positions in Saudi Aramco (as the company is now known).

> "my family and I love the people, the culture, the weather (yes, the weather), the sights and the ambience."

I moved on to other jobs in Mobil in 1984, but came back to Saudi Arabia in 1988, when I was appointed Chairman and CEO of Mobil Saudi Arabia, Inc. I was based in Jeddah, where I lived with my family. This opened up a new dimension to my Saudi Arabian experience. Living in the Kingdom is very different from trips in and out, even though these trips may have been frequent and extended over many years. I remained in Jeddah until 1993.

It was a wonderful time for my family and me. We met many new friends, Saudi and expatriate. We experienced the joys of Jeddah, as well as the other cities of Saudi Arabia; the desert, and the Red Sea. My family and I especially enjoyed boating on the Red Sea, also the snorkeling and scuba diving. We were all very sad to leave Jeddah for a new assignment in the US in 1993.

However, like many others we found out that you cannot stay away from Saudi Arabia for long. I was reassigned to Saudi Arabia in June 1998 as Chairman and CEO, Mobil Saudi Arabia Inc. This time around my family and I are living in Riyadh. We are looking forward to the opportunity to meet new friends, and more closely experience.

Saudi Arabia gets into one's blood. My family and I love the people, the culture, the weather (yes, the weather), the sights and the ambience. In our minds, there is no place like it. The memories will be cherished forever.

 Curtis W. Brand is an American. He is the Chairman and CEO of Mobil Saudi Arabia Inc. He has been living in the Kingdom for five years.

A Pure Way Of Life

BY: ADAM CHARLES EL ENANY

audi Arabia is not the only country I've lived in, but it is one of the finest places I have had the privilege of living in.

It is a focal point for all the nationalities of the world, especially within its two holy cities of Makkah and Madina. Riyadh is a cosmopolitan city of high-rise buildings, large department stores and parks that dot the capital like spots on a leopard. But getting away from all the physical aspects of Riyadh and moving to probably the most important characteristic of any country in the world–its people.

The Saudis are not only good, kind-hearted people, but the most helpful I've ever encountered. They are the first to help in situations such as when my father's car broke down a few months ago.

While my father was steering, I was having a lot of trouble pushing our four-wheeler. Suddenly, it felt as if I was pushing a dust ball! It was then, to my surprise, that I realised that there were two Saudi youths helping me, one on each side of me. Some might think that they were merely the odd two good doers, but no, that wasn't the case.

" It has compelled me to decide that when I have children someday in the future, I shall return to the Kingdom with them and place them in the same clean, pure and ideal environment that I have been exposed to ".

Just a couple of days ago, the car in which my mother was being driven in with her friend broke down in the middle of a highway. Within no time some Saudis came to their assistance and finally got the car started once more.

Some people ask me, why do you go on living here when you can live somewhere like England? I tell them that is because Saudi Arabia forbids every kind of evil such as intoxication, murder, burglary, vandalism, homosexuality and drug abuse, whereas most other countries are filled with all these, maintain no strict punishments and have little control over them.

Living in a country like Saudi Arabia has not only sustained my morals but also preserved my childhood and purified my heart. It has compelled me to decide that when I have children someday in the future, I shall return to the Kingdom with them and place them in the same clean, pure and ideal environment that I have been exposed to.

 Adam Charles El Enany is from Britain, he is a student and has been living in the Kingdom for 11 years.

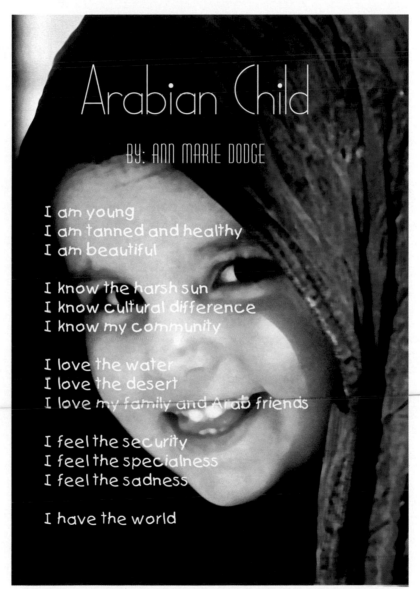

Arabian Child

BY: ANN MARIE DODGE

I am young
I am tanned and healthy
I am beautiful

I know the harsh sun
I know cultural difference
I know my community

I love the water
I love the desert
I love my family and Arab friends

I feel the security
I feel the specialness
I feel the sadness

I have the world

*Ann wrote this poem when she
was ten years old in 1983*

THE KINGDOM'S FAR-REACHING EFFECT

BY: AHMED PHILIP HUNT

I first came to Saudi Arabia in 1978. I have been employed in many towns and cities throughout the Kingdom and have visited many others. To best evaluate the enormous progress and changes that have taken place it is necessary to make periodic visits to places you have previously been to. My first post in the Kingdom was in Riyadh. At the time Riyadh was being referred to by the Western media as "the World's biggest building site".

What was most striking was the daily appearance of hundreds of industrial "hard-hatted" workers in almost every part of the city. The skyline was one of giant cranes, the noise of earth-moving equipment was everywhere. The old airport in Riyadh was the point of entry for most people coming to Riyadh. The magnificent new airport was under construction. The Diplomatic Quarter was still on the drawing board. One enormous building after another was springing up almost overnight. The time was the so-called boom period. Little did we know that we were on the brink of a worldwide recession.

Two outstanding events took place during my years in Riyadh. One was the opening of the Military Hospital by the late King Khaled, and the second a visit to the hospital by Queen Elizabeth and Prince Philip.

My second visit to Saudi Arabia was a couple of years later. It was to Yanbu that I came this time. That was my very best year in Saudi Arabia. It was the year in which I was able to buy my own house in England and completely furnish it. Sadly it was the start of the recession in Europe and the beginning of the end of the so-called boom years in Saudi Arabia. Yanbu was a "hard hat" city too. It was very quickly becoming the model industrial city it is today. I think just about every nationality in the world was represented in Yanbu. Every morning on my way to work I would see hundreds of workmen's bus convoys commuting the industrial sites.

After a very short period at home I returned to Saudi Arabia to take up a new appointment in a small village called Afif. It was one of the most relaxed villages I had ever been to. There was the usual supermarket, petrol station, fire station, police station, telephone exchange, post office , hospital and school all in one main street. What I enjoyed there was the freedom of countryside walks, rocky hill climbs and the simplicity of life style. From Afif I moved to Hail. The country walks and the rock climbs around. Hail are magical. Just to get away from work and climb up to the mountains was a rest cure all on its own. Hail was under development, so some parts of the town were old, some ancient, and some extremely modern .

From Hail I moved to Majmah. Although I was there only for a few months I got to know the place well with the help of my new found Saudi friends. In all the places I have been to in Saudi Arabia I have found the friendliness and hospitality of the Saudis to be extraordinary. Even when I was out on my country walks I would receive offers of tea,coffee or cool drinks by complete strangers. Sometimes I would be invited to take a meal or given guided tours of farms

and ancient ruins. Nothing ever seemed to be too much trouble for the Saudis I met.

I became a Muslim about five years ago, and to say that I was treated like a long lost brother on his return would be an understatement. To the Saudi, the brotherhood of Islam is almost always seen as an obligation. Together with their cultural extension of friendship and generosity, a new Muslim can feel a bit overwhelmed. My only regret is that I didn't become a Muslim in 1978.

I have spent my last 7 years in Jeddah. Jeddah is a city of so many complexities and extremes. The Saudi friends I have met here have taken great delight and pride in showing me their city.

It is unfortunate that most Western visitors will never get to see Makkah or Madina. Makkah is a place of warm and kind people, yet because of its importance to Islam and its cramped situation in a small valley, it always appears overcrowded, and in a hurry.

Madina is a complete contrast with its wide open

spaces and high rise buildings. One place you really should visit in Saudi Arabia is Taif. Who can say though which is the best place to visit. I have enjoyed all the places I have been to.

"In all the places I have been to in Saudi Arabia I have found the friendliness and hospitality of the Saudis to be extraordinary. Even when I was out on my country walks I would receive offers of tea, coffee or cool drinks by complete strangers."

One of the most important aspects of Saudi Arabia, perhaps missed by most people, is the effect Saudi development has had on the lives of untold millions of people throughout the world. Not only has the Kingdom provided well paid jobs to people from every corner of the globe, but through trade it has generated work for millions more. I am happy to see Saudi Arabia achieving self-sufficiency in so many ways.

When I first came to Saudi Arabia unemployment in Europe had reached 12 million. If it hadn't been for that chance to come here my dreams would never have come true. I think there must be millions of expatriates from around the world who can say the same thing. Now, my dreams are fulfilled, and I pray that the visions that Saudi Arabia holds will bear fruit, and that I will still be here to see that day.

 Ahmed Philip Hunt is British. He is a Nursing Equipment and Supplies Coordinator with Rajab-Silsilah, and has been living in the Kingdom for 20 years.

From American To Saudi-American

By: H. Kenneth Palmer

THE Palmers arrived in the Kingdom's Eastern Province in 1985–my wife, Patricia, leaving a highly successful career as an artist and costume designer, and myself fresh from international corporate banking.

Like many expatriates, we figured on a couple of years in the Kingdom and then back to our "real life". Thirteen exciting and fruitful years later, having moved from the East to Jeddah and then to Riyadh, our "real world" is Saudi Arabia, complete with many rewarding personal, professional and artistic relationships.

It's always about the people. No exception here. Our life has been rich with Saudi and expatriate friends from all walks of life and all parts of the Kingdom and the globe. We've worked hard to develop Saudi friendships and both mine and Patricia's works have given us a helpful head start.

Art has a common vocabulary and it often transcends cultural boundaries. As an artist, Patricia has ready access to Saudi women artists who are always eager to reach out and associate with a fellow artist. They discuss art and share work techniques. Some of them work in different mediums–photography, sculpture, ceramics, to name a few, but they all share the common language of creativity. Through the years, Patricia has particularly enjoyed seeing many of her friends grow and mature in their artistic expression and individuality.

I've worked in senior positions in the National Commercial Bank, Riyad Bank and Whinney Murray, and my office and market relationships have been very full and rewarding. I've been around long enough to know the ropes, and have met many people from different walks of life. As we moved companies and changed locations we gained new friends but did not give up the old. One of them is Fahad Al-Muaibid and his family whom we first met in the Eastern

Province in 1985. We've seen their children grow up, new babies arrive, and no doubt we will be there for future weddings. I for sure want to be around when Fahad becomes a grandfather for the first time.

Life for us Palmers changed as we settled into our Saudi lifestyles. Patricia's art flourished and she produces wonderful paintings and collages inspired by Old Jeddah, Saudi wild flowers, Bedouin arts, and the pre-history of Arabia. With her long list of Saudi and expatriate clients, she is highly regarded in the art community here. She usually holds an annual exhibition, and has also appeared on television.

My lifelong interest and involvement with nature blos-

somed here and we are constant off-road travellers throughout the wonderful, wide-open Saudi landscape. All over the world people are nostalgic for elbow room, freedom of movement. Not here, where one can drive for hundreds of kilometres in some of the most spectacular settings on earth with only occasional human encounters. The Rub Al-Khali is a favourite destination and we have crossed it several times. We carry all the necessary desert equipment, including intrepid friends willing to undertake this kind of adventure.

Where are the personal rewards? For me, they have been in my involvement with young Saudis whom I have had the good fortune to mentor. Time and again I have seen bright young men stretch, meet the challenge, and move on from strength to strength. These men and others like them are part of a strong national fabric and it is my privilege to have been involved, even if only in a small way, with their success.

Wherever and however we live, there is value in changing our perspective; and life in another culture forces shifts in our individual paradigms. Through our life here, we have developed a Saudi-American perspective and our life is richer because of the ways we have refocused our lives. While there is never enough time, a new reality for us has been that we have slowed down enough to enjoy the journey and savour the moments of our life.

 H.Kenneth Palmer is an American,he works for Whinney Murray & Co. in Riyadh as an Executive Director, Bank Training Services, he has been living in the Kingdom for 13 years.

my JEW

BY: MIKE CROCKER

arriving in the land of Saud as a boy of two in 1951, I came to love the desert and the beauty of the Arab way of life. I grew up protected, by both the oil company and the Saudi government, but my playmates and friends were Saudis my age. They taught me many things: the cruelty of the desert, the beauty of the night, the blessings God gave to Arabia and to me. I was taught the Arabs were an inferior race, because they were so backward, but in reality their ways were years ahead of my own people. I watched a beheading when I was very small. I met with King Faisal, and had tea with Ibn Jawuli. They that taught me right from wrong in ways that guide me to this day and, like the ships of the desert, my Bedouin friends taught me never to be lost and always be among friends.

The oil company gave me the finest in education, the Saudis the finest in honour and respect. Loyalty and fidelity I learned in a tent in the Rub Al-Khali. I learned to master an Arabian stallion at the age of 12 and rode the winds of Arabia along the shores of Azzizia.

I knew all was not what it may have seemed, but the majesty of the Arab world was but an opera for me. Saudi justice was swift, but the Quran was the law, and the law was the rule, and the King was the keeper of the law.

the Saudis the finest in honour and respect."

Friendships made and brothers lost only made Saudi Arabia more my home than the flag of my birth. In my years, Ibn Saud passed on and Prince Faisal led his people and along the way he led me. When his heart stopped, the sands of the desert seemed to stop their movement, in honour and respect for this great man among men. The Flower of Arabia so cruelly cut down...he who had brought his people into the light. My own tears and my Saudi friends' tears were one and the same. King Faisal was my John F. Kennedy, both rulers of the people, not by force of arms but by force of love within their hearts.

You ask me about growing up in Saudi Arabia, and grow I did. In my opinion Arabia today is

83

not the Arabia of the Lion, but progress has changed all of us. We are now the old Bedu who studies the black ribbon across the desert that we today call a road. Progress we must, but under the King, it must be just (as a child, I knew this, and as a man I respect). Although an infidel I have shed blood in the desert and have studied the Holy Writings, and find that I, a mere child of Arabia, have become a man of the sand. The courtesy of the Arab and the belief of the faithful are lessons we non-Arab peoples could and should learn. I, growing up in Saudi Arabia, was truly blessed by God.

 Former Aramco employee

Saudi Women At Work

BY: HELEN KIRKPATRICK HENRY

The highlight of my life in Saudi Arabia are the years I worked at a Training Center for Saudi women at one of the local hospitals. During this period I had the opportunity to work with, and get to know, over a hundred Saudi women.

When the pilot project began some of these women, between the ages of 18 and 25, had very few English language skills. This made it difficult for them, as most of the staff spoke little or no Arabic and all the curricula were in English. But the students were eager to overcome this hurdle and learn their chosen profession of either Nursing or Health Records Administration.

The Western consultants from the United Kingdom and Canada were most impressed with how quickly our students mastered the English language and developed critical thinking skills, which are essential when learning a course based on Western standards. Even though during the first year I taught math and science, I explained to the students that I was really teaching them English as well as how to transfer knowledge.

The first time I gave a math test with problems they had never seen before, the students were shocked. When I explained that the problems were the same kind as those they had worked out in the class, they were a little more confident of their ability. This was another hurdle the women overcame.

The expatriate consultant from the Ministry of Health who helped develop the curriculum was most impressed with our students' dedication. They were also equally committed to their families, especially their children, yet they still managed to be at he Training Center every day by 7.30 a.m, when classes began.

Many of these women got married, pregnant,

and had children during the course. They made up for the work they missed during the absence and graduated with their classmates. I was so very proud of the first class of 63 students who completed all the graduation requirements. I had seen these young women overcome many hardships to reach their goal.

Although I was unable to continue with the program, I remain in contact with some of my students. They are pursuing their professions, as well as taking care of their children and families.

I vividly remember my time with these young women and wish them all the best. If any of them happen to read this article, I hope they know that I admire them for their accomplishments. I consider myself very fortunate to have had the opportunity to know and teach these Saudi women.

 Helen Kirkpatrick Henry is an American, she is the Director of American Community Services and has been in the Kingdom for six years.

Where is Saudi Arabia Anyway?

By: Jack H. West

When my company, Fluor Daniel, asked me in 1982 if I could consider a transfer to Jeddah, Saudi Arabia, the first thing that came to my mind was, exactly where is Saudi Arabia?

I'm from the small town of Fountain Inn, South Carolina (population 5,000) and had never considered living abroad, much less Saudi Arabia. After several sleepless nights, I made the decision to give it a try.

On the flight from Greenville to New York, the thought was always in my mind that I can still get on the next flight back home, but once I boarded the Saudi flight, reality began to hit me. As the Saudia 747 lifted off from the JFK, I thought to myself, "What have I done? I'm going to Saudi Arabia for several years and don't know anything about the country, the people, or their culture".

During the eight years (three different tours) that I have been in Jeddah, I have learned much about the Saudi people and their customs and have developed many long lasting friendships. The Saudis, once you have gained their trust, are true friends that you can depend to assist with any problems that you encounter. They will go out of the way to assist you and never expect anything in return. Once I depart the Kingdom next year, I will dearly miss my friends here but look forward to their visiting me in the States and I welcome the opportunity to return the hospitality that was shown to me here.

"As the Saudia 747 lifted off
from JFK, I thought to myself, What
I have done!!!"

Since my arrival in 1983, I have witnessed the growth and development of the Kingdom. I have personally been involved with the King Abdul Aziz University Health Sciences Centre Project in Jeddah, the expansion of the Rabigh Power Station, Phase IV in Rabigh, and the Yanpet Petrochemical Expansion Project in Yanbu. All of

these facilities will assist the Kingdom in achieving their social and economic goals.

The Kingdom has many diverse and interesting sites to offer that many expatriates never see just because they don't take the time or make an effort to see them. The Hijaz Railway Station and the tombs of the

Nebateans at Mada'in Saleh are two of the most interesting sites that you will see anywhere. The waterfall between Jeddah and Taif is very interesting and the drive to the top of the mountain is an experience in itself. Another interesting site is the crater that is between Taif and Riyadh. The areas of Najran and Abha are also very interesting and the drive is breathtaking. The old section of Jeddah and the Nasif House are just as intriguing. One must make time to visit some of these areas to get a better understanding of the Kingdom and its people.

I have also enjoyed the friendships that I have made with other expatriates from various countries throughout the world. All in all, it has been a great experience that I will always remember. I feel that I have a better understanding of the world in general and a better appreciation for what I have taken for granted at home in the United States.

I would highly recommend to anyone that if offered the opportunity to work and live in the Kingdom, take the chance. You will find the experience very rewarding, both financially and personally.

 Jack H. West is an American, he has been living in the Kingdom for eight years, he works as Sr. Manager, Human Resources with Fluor Daniel Arabia.

Going Back Through Time

By: Carmen Florea Wilhelm

There is so much history in the Kingdom of Saudi Arabia. Being here I have had the opportunity to witness things first-hand, which otherwise I would only have read about in books.

We have visited many famous and unique places in the Kingdom, and I will always treasure the memories. On our visit to the Asir Region, standing on top of the magnificent and cool mountain, I could almost recapture the picture of the ancient merchants as they trekked through the frankincense route, laden with riches from the Far East. I felt as if I were transported back through time to that historic moment.

There is something in their milieu which I long for. I wonder about the ancient Nabataean civilisation which started in Mada'in Saleh and extended its culture to what is now Petra in Jordan. I wish that I could have experienced it first hand.

A trip to the south-western part of the Kingdom in Asir brought us to the "Hanging village" of Habalah. We listened in awe as the tour guide explained how the people who once lived in the village descended and ascended it by means of a simple rope. He also explained how its unique but precarious position

served as a natural fortification from enemies. Gradually they were persuaded for safety reasons to leave their village permanently, and take up residence in a nearby village constructed specifically for them.

Tourism has been developing in the Kingdom because of the many wonderful and fascinating places to visit. On several occasions, we have had our sons

over from the United States, and they were able to enjoy those things unique to Saudi Arabia, such as camping in the desert as well as other worldly pleasures such as water skiing, scuba diving, hiking, etc.

During a brief return to the United States, between assignments here in Saudi Arabia, I was very excited to be given the opportunity to take Social Studies classes for American students. I could give them up, close and personal accounts of some of the places we had visited such as Jeddah, the Red Sea, the Arabian Gulf, Abha, Khamis Mushayt and many other cities in Egypt, Jordan, Oman, and Syria. In addition, I was able to share with them the photographs, tapes and souvenirs that we had collected over our many years in the Kingdom.

In summary, living in the Kingdom has been a grand experience and one for which I am truly grateful. In addition to those things mentioned earlier, the people are wonderful and very kind and generous. I have had the opportunity to meet several lovely Saudi ladies who have become dear friends of mine. Also, we have become close friends with a Saudi family

and enjoy a relationship with them much the same as we could expect to find back in the United States.

 Carmen Florea Wilheim is a teacher from the U.S. She has been living in the Kingdom for seven years.

Teasing The King

BY: CARLA CHERWINSKI WOODCOCK

My journey to Saudi Arabia began long before I could begin to comprehend and appreciate the vast beauty and deep mysteries of this ancient kingdom. Through a child's eyes, what might have seemed strange and exotic, appeared natural and comforting. In truth, it was home. With the passing of many years, I am left with an amazing dream of what was my early life's greatest adventure.

Through the memories of my parents, Bette and Carl Cherwinski, I am able to relate to you a brief moment in time when I crossed paths with a king, King Abdul Aziz Ibn Saud, in September of 1954. I was three and a half years old and have only this old photograph to recall the event. Surrounded by princes, statesmen and representatives of Aramco, King Abdul Aziz paid a visit to Dhahran. Studying the photograph, I am struck by what must have been a warm and open atmosphere amongst the people gathered in front of the Hamilton House, despite the seriousness of an appearance by the King of Saudi Arabia.

As tiny as I was, I was able to slip through the ranks to deliver a handful of flowers to the King. When he bent down to accept the bouquet, I tucked them out of reach behind my back. To his credit, this man of imposing stature laughed!

Today, I would never presume to approach a King uninvited. I would surely be discrete, respectful, at a distance. But, what a delightful gift is this memory, a fleeting moment of humour, bridging the gap between the mighty and the small. Throughout my life, an enlarged copy of this photo has had its place in my home. Friends and relatives have remarked on its unusual content and smiled on hearing the story. It serves as a reminder of a time when ordinary people like me had the tremendous opportunity to experience extraordinary things, a time when the world felt smaller, yet filled with adventure.

" When the King bent down to accept
the bouquet, I tucked them out of reach
behind my back. To his credit, this man
of imposing stature laughed!"

 Former Aramco employee

A Geological Plate

BY: ANTHEA HELEN HATFIELD

For me it was traffic problems. One more demerit point and they would take my driver's license away. Why not work in a country that would not even let me drive a car at all?

I am an anesthetist and I have worked here at the Military Hospital for 16 months. I love it, no car, that big heap of expensive metal that got me into so much trouble. And instead of driving miles from one hospital to another and coming home late at night, all my work is now on one campus. I finish in time to swim every day. I lie in my pool, staring up at the brilliant blue sky fringed with bright pink bougainvillaea, and wonder why I didn't come years ago, why I didn't leave the rat race I was in and come to Saudi Arabia.

My previous life, though not even two years ago,

seems far away. In those days, I could not have told you which was the Gulf and which was the Red Sea. I was always a little confused when referring to Iran and Iraq. As for the Palestinian and Israeli conflict, I was ignorant. I now have a reasonable good idea of the geography of the region. I understand something of Islam, as well as the ancient history of Arabia. I have been to Abha and looked down from the high cliffs to see the old camel trails winding up from the sea. In Jeddah I have walked through the streets of the ancient city which are almost exactly as they looked in old photographs of the twenties and thirties. I have driven along the corniche and seen the beautiful white mosques.

I have visited Mada'in Saleh with the Nebataean tombs; as though we were driving through a sunken mountain range, perhaps an ancient fiord system from millions of years ago.

Around Riyadh the scenery and geology are also dramatic. Saudi Arabia must be a geological plate, sloping down from the Red Sea and arising again somewhere under Iran (which would

"I lie in my pool, staring up at the brilliant blue sky fringed with bright pink bougainvillaea, and wonder why I didn't come years ago."

explain the stability here and earthquakes there). Many parts of the Riyadh district must have once been under the sea. I have climbed under the escarpments and found fossilized sea eggs, shells and coral.

I came to Saudi Arabia, knowing nothing of what was here and have found riches to enjoy far beyond my expectations. We have young Saudi doctors and technicians in our department who are a real delight to teach and who make a huge effort to reach high standards. One of our doctors is already famous, being the first Saudi to pass the Saudi Board's examination in anesthesia. All this is so rewarding and marvellous to be part of. I feel proud to make a contribution and very pleased that my bad driving, which was my reason to come here in the first place, would not even be noticed here as everyone else is so much worse.

 Anthea Helen Hatfield is from New Zealand. She is a doctor at the Military Hospital, Riyadh, and has been living in the Kingdom for one year and four months.

The Bedouin Coffee Ritual

By: Monroe Pastermack

I had come to Saudi Arabia to visit my parents and learn more about entomology, but something more important happened to this 21 year-old college student from the United States. One hot and humid July day in 1956, in the oasis of Al-Hofuf in the Eastern Province (Al-Hasa) Saudi Arabia, the four of us, Muhammad, Samir, George and I, (the only American) had just completed our "mosquito collecting" for the Aramco Medical Department.

There we were in the middle of this lush date palm forest desperate for something cool to drink, when the owner of the farm rode up on his horse and asked us to come to his house for coffee. As he led the way through the rows of date palms the farmer proudly described each type of date, and Muhammad translated for me. Upon entering the courtyard of the stone and brick main house, I could see a small open fire surrounded by palm logs arranged around the fire. The log circle was in the shade of the house. Seated in front of the fire was a very old man who greeted us with a smile and a welcome. We were asked to sit and enjoy the cool shade and we were further cooled through the warmth of their hospitality.

The old man began chanting, in what sounded to me like poetry. Muhammad translated as quickly as he could and I discovered the elder was quoting from The Holy Quran. The sounds and the rhythm was beautiful. He then set about making coffee in the traditional Bedouin manner, first roasting the beans in a *mihmas*, and then beating out a wondrous melody on the mortar and pestle grinding the coffee, as he sang along. As the coffee was flavoured with both cardamom and saffron, I knew we were special guests. With each of the six cups of fragrant coffee, there was talk of health and prosperity for all present and for the families of those present.

" Forty one years later I try to treat all strangers, particularly people from other cultures and countries, with the hospitality and dignity I learned in an oasis in Saudi Arabia"

"Why are you in Saudi Arabia?"
"I'm visiting my parents."
"May Allah bring peace and health to your parents."
"Why are you here in our oasis?"
"I'm working to help rid the oasis of mosquitoes and disease."
"May Allah bring you good fortune for helping others."

Through the Bedouin coffee ritual our cultures touched in a beautiful way and for a moment in time, I felt accepted as part of the Saudi culture.

Sitting in my house in Oakland, California, reminiscent of my days in Saudi Arabia, I think back to being on a farm in the Al-Hofuf

oasis listening to a beautiful melody being beaten out on the *yud alhawand* (brass mortar and pestle). Often, when I grind my coffee each day, I think of that time in the past when I fully experienced Bedouin hospitality. In my mind's eye, I see the six of us sitting around the open fire sharing coffee and each other's company. Forty-one years later I try to treat all strangers, particularly people from other cultures and countries, with the hospitality and dignity I learned in an oasis in Saudi Arabia.

 Former Aramco employee

Peace At Last

By: Mohammed Randy Horton

My coming to Saudi Arabia has indeed been a blessing. It was here that I was introduced to Islam, the religion I eventually embraced. I can say that my experience with Islamic beliefs, as well as my friendships with Saudis has made me a better person.

I have also become a much more secure person. Before coming to Saudi Arabia with my family I was always gripped by constant fear of criminal incidents, a rampant occurrence in the other countries I was in. Here, I have only witnessed a peaceful life where I can walk in the streets in the middle of the night without fear.

My fondest memory of the Kingdom however, is my conversion to Islam. It has opened up for me a whole new way of looking at things. I have become more generous, understanding and peace-loving as a result of my conversion. I have also become more tolerant of the inadequacies of others. Generosity is another aspect that I like about the Muslims. The sight of so many people offering food to friends and total strangers alike during the holy month of Ramadan is for me the height of humane participation.

There are other things too for which I have come to like Saudi Arabia. Its deserts are indeed a good place to go to for an experience that is totally different from life in the capital city. This unique side of nature with stretches of uninhabited land dotted with clumps of date trees in the broad expanse of desert is one that I could hardly trade for any other. Driving along valleys and sand dunes as a family, we feel a sense of togetherness. It's during those moments when I can feel that we, my Filipina wife and two children, are indeed a close family intact and one.

When we come back to the city after a few days of absence, and take a plunge into the swimming pool at the back of the house, I reflect that we could never undergo the experience we enjoy here in any other country. My family agrees with me.

 Mohammed Randy Horton is from the U.S. He is a customer care manager at Motorola.

RESPECT THE ENVIRONMENT

BY: DAMIAN JAMES

bviously, as a Western expatriate, the ways of life here are different from my own back home, but that's no bad thing. I think diversity of culture and tradition is one of the many remarkable learning experiences in life. It provides a truer perspective of the world in which we live.

These are interesting times and the Kingdom continues to develop at a considerable pace. I am a senior manager employed with one of the world's leading international public relations agencies. Over the years we have provided the gateway for many international clients who want to conduct business here and communicate at a local level, and for Saudi companies who want to gain international exposure through our global network.

Professionally, it is a very challenging and rewarding environment. Being able to advise our clients on local considerations and the ever challenging developments are an important part of the service we provide.

But it's not all work–I am a keen diver and the many wonders of the Red Sea provide some of the best diving experiences in the world. I have also enjoyed some "wadi-bashing" and have explored the escarpment up and around Taif which provide some truly amazing scenery.

Saudi Arabia is a country with a rich, diverse natural countryside that is available for anyone who wants to go beyond their compound. Obviously, you have to be aware that the environment can be very unforgiving and should be treated with respect at all times.

 Damian James is a British national. He is a Senior Manager of a PR firm, and has been living in the Kingdom for one year and six months.

The Crooked House

By: Jean F. de St. Croix

My husband arrived in Saudi Arabia in 1951, our children were raised there. It was the most wounderful period of our lives.

In the late 60's and early 70's the government was increasing encouragement for Saudis to go into business—open small factories, build things, become entrepreneurs. Our family had just moved from a small house in Dhahran to a beautiful stone free–standing house which had a huge picture window overlooking the back patio. This showed evidence of previous occupations brick, rubble, and a partly submerged concrete block with a mound in the center which might have been a barbecue pit. Metal reinforcing rods stuck out, and one side was smashed down.

It was a dangerous mess. We decided to remove it and build a patio in its place. Our friend Hassan knew a man in Qatif who had a cousin whose wife's brother was now in the tile business and had recently opened a tile factory in Al-Khobar. By word of mouth an appointment with Muhammad was made. He arrived, stated that he could do the job as he had already worked on two patios, and asked whether we would like to see his factory.

The plant was in Al-Khobar and was indeed turning out beautiful concrete patio tiles with multi-colored stone. We could have any color we wanted. It was agreed that Muhammad would clear the rubble and construct a new patio to be the length of the house, about 60 feet long, and 20 feet wide with a 3 foot wide space between the patio and the house, for flowers and bushes.

Soon trucks lined the alley. Hammers chopped the rubble and hauled it away. A cement mixer, piles of desert sand, stacks of tile and boards filled the alley. Three days later a proud Muhammad knocked on my door and announced, "Finished! Come see".

It was beautiful, perfect. I was truly pleased. Muhammad stood straight and tall as my neighbors "oohed" and "aahed" and congratulated us both on the new addition. However, something was wrong, something was just not right, but what? Finally I noticed. "Look Muhammad . This end of the patio is 3 feet from the house. That's good. But the other end of the patio is only I foot from the house. Not enough room for flowers. What happened?"

Well, Muhammad knew the patio was right, well done, and that I liked it. He walked up and down, staring at the narrowing strip of garden between it and the house. It could not be that his work was wrong. Certainly a Saudi contractor knows more about patios than an Aramco housewife, and Muhammad was not about to lose face.

Finally the problem was solved. Muhammad looked at me with those gorgeous penetrating eyes, smiled, flashing his gold tooth and announced. "Mrs, your house is crooked!"

A Lesson Of Experience

By: Jean Ko Ko Gyo

Before arriving in Saudi Arabia my thoughts were of a country with very strict and overwhelming rules and regulations. After arriving in the Kingdom I began to understand that this is a developing country with strict and strong, but simple, traditional values. For me to see a Saudi family having a picnic by the road side is an interesting and touching scene.

The people here are also known for their generous hospitality. I had been in Riyadh for just a few months, when one of our patients invited the whole Radiation-Therapy Department and Dental Clinic to his farm to spend the day on a weekend. The patient was very generous and hospitable. We had a meal that included a whole roasted baby camel, and a mountain of fruits and sweets. It was spectacular, as well as delicious.

> " What amazes me is that I can travel at night with thousands of riyals in my purse, without fear. This is something I wouldn't dream of doing in any other part of the world".

The same year one of the Saudi girls from the hospital got married and I was invited along with my roommate and some of our friends. That occasion is one memory of Saudi Arabia that I will always treasure. The event was mixed with culture and tradition, and I was thrilled to be part of it.

The best thing I like about Saudi Arabia is the ensured security. It is an unbelievable experience to go shopping down to the gold *souq* (market) on a bus in the middle of a night, during Ramadan. The festive spirit of night shopping is truly infectious. What amazes me is that I can travel at night with thousands of riyals in my purse, without fear. This is something I wouldn't dream of doing in any other part of the world.

Another benefit of being here is that I have learned

a lot about history, geography, religion and language of different parts of the world. I have also noticed the different usages of English by those who speak it as the first language such as the Americans, British, Canadians, Australians and New Zealanders. It is interesting and educational.

As an American citizen, the rest of the world seemed so far away, until I came to Saudi Arabia. After coming here I have travelled to Egypt, Europe and Asia, more miles than ever before in my life. Definitely, the one lesson you cannot get in a classroom or from the text book is the lesson of experience.

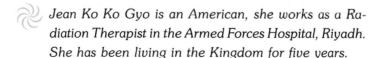 *Jean Ko Ko Gyo is an American, she works as a Radiation Therapist in the Armed Forces Hospital, Riyadh. She has been living in the Kingdom for five years.*

Coping With A New Environment

By: Saifuddin B. C. Thassim

Eighteen years is a long time to spend in a foreign country, that too working all that while for one company. I have moved with people belonging to different nationalities, races and cultures, and have worked closely with a variety of men, numbering more than 52. I can quote, quite copiously, my varied experiences in the Kingdom. However I shall restrict myself to just a few. As expatriates, we go through a traumatic experience coming to an alien country, leaving our loved ones far behind. The age limit for employment in Saudi is 22 years and above. After living for that many years in his own country and then switching to a new environment will undoubtedly result in some problems. Sacrifices do arise. Home-sickness coupled with the difficulties of adjusting to a new environment may even lead to complete frustration.

In such a frame of mind it is natural that some expatriates do not take to the surroundings at all. Finding it stressful to adjust, they tend to complain at everything. Nothing can meet their satisfaction, whatever the circumstance. For such type of people my sincere advice would be to leave the Kingdom.

I believe that one should cultivate the habit of recognising and appreciating the good things in life, and be grateful to a country that earns you your daily bread and butter.

My experiences in the Kingdom are numerous some can be termed as nasty, and still some are acceptable, but most of them reflect the overall kind-heartedness of the Saudis.

Most of us would have experienced the considerate nature of the Saudis who rush to the assistance of motorists stranded in the road's ways. Recently during the height of summer at 1 p.m. I was on the hot roads in the midst of heavy slow-moving traffic, when suddenly my vehicle came to an abrupt halt. My wife was sitting by

my side and I did not know what to do. Alarming beeps from fellow motorists started upsetting me. Coupled with traffic jam, everyone was in a rush to reach home for lunch, or to schools to pick their children. To them, I was indeed a nuisance.

Practically everyone passing me was displaying undisguised resentment. I felt very much the unwanted expatriate in the midst of everyone. Then to my utter surprise a car slowed down by my side. The Saudi driver signaled to me that he would

turn around the roundabout I was stranded in and return. Soon he was behind me in his vehicle with which he pushed my car to a safe place. He then left without even expecting a "thank you." This action touched my heart and my inner sense thanked him profusely.

Another time, 10 years ago, I was returning from Madina when my car broke down in the middle of the desert. We left the car in a nearby garage and an expatriate driver offered to take us to Qassim on payment of a

100 riyals each. Half-way through the journey he stopped the vehicle stating that he wanted to stay overnight in the desert, to which we did not agree. We had an argument and finally handed over 200 riyals for the short distance we had travelled in his car. A passing Saudi stopped his vehicle, saw our predicament, and without any financial benefit helped us to reach Qassim.

One cannot expect everything to be perfect in an alien country, and we should learn to adjust ourselves to the conditions prevailing. Only then can we enjoy the goodwill of all concerned.

 Saifuddin Thassim is a Sri Lankan He is a Senior Manager at the Saudi American Bank. He has been living in the Kingdom for 18 years.

CALL TO PRAYER

BY: GARY R. ANSORGE

In the summer of 1990, I was working for SCECO in Dhahran, Saudi Arabia as an electronics technician. One of the Saudis I worked with was Saib Al-Ghamdi, an intelligent, educated gentleman who had been in the Saudi navy. He was educated in the United States for several years. His command of English was truly excellent and we had many interesting discussions about the similarities and differences between our two cultures. He was also religious and tried very hard to stimulate my interest in Islam. He had some success but I was not at that time ready to give deep consideration to something I could only dimly comprehend. I did, however, listen to him.

This story is not however, about Saib.

On a hot, sultry summer day in 1990, I had taken my car to Al-Khobar to have some repairs done that I could not perform myself. As I was waiting for the work to be done I was idly thinking about some of my conversations with my friend Saib concerning the unity of man under God, when a *mutawa'a* in a truck came down the dusty road, announcing the call to prayer. It was time to close up the shop for prayers.

Most Americans are, I know, somewhat put out when prayer call interferes with work we think important. Here I was, dressed in my typical Thursday attire of jeans and brightly coloured tie-dyed T-shirt, sporting all the colours of the rainbow, while this very proper and serious Saudi Arab was calling my business to a halt. As he drove past me I waved at him and smiled, for I knew his faith was more important than my business.

To my surprise, he turned his head my way, smiled a brilliant smile, and waved back. It was then I knew the old adage was true. If you make *eye* contact with an Arab, it is said, he will be your friend for life. Thus I was assured, we really are all one family under God.

Touched In The Tihama

By: Brad Davis

My interest in the Middle East began when I was studying for my undergraduate degree in engineering at Dartmouth College. It was there that I met a doctoral candidate who offered to conduct basic Arabic lessons for a small group of interested students. Upon completion of my Masters Degree in Engineering Sciences, I was awarded a Rotary Scholarship to study Arabic language and culture at the American University in Cairo. That was more then 10 years ago, and my affection for the Middle East has only grown stronger since then.

During my tenure in Riyadh, I have met some wonderful people, both Saudi and expatriate. The Kingdom brings together a collection of

" There is so much more to the
Kingdom than the stereotypical
images of desert, which
unfortunately is all that most
people at home think of when we
mention Saudi Arabia."

nationalities, and it is a remarkable opportunity to be able to associate with and learn from persons from all corners of the globe. I enjoy the more personal touch to life, which we in the U.S. seem to have lost to a great degree, but which is still very much alive in the Kingdom. People still take the time here to exchange greetings, inquire about the family, and show hospitality to the visitor.

There is also an element of trust and honesty which one would be hard pressed to find in other parts of the world. Where else would a carpet store urge the customer to bring home a very expensive Oriental carpet to try out for a few days? It is a very safe and secure environment that the Kingdom provides, and I feel comfortable walking down any street in Riyadh at any time of the day or night. I cannot make that claim for many places in my own country.

One of the nicest experiences I have had in the Kingdom was during the Ramadan Eid period of 1997. My parents were visiting me for the first time, and a friend and I had planned a trip by car around the Kingdom that took us from Riyadh to Abha, up past

Al-Baha and Taif to Jeddah, and back to Riyadh. My parents were incredibly surprised at the variety of landscapes they encountered, and agreed that there is so much more to the Kingdom than the stereotypical images of desert, which unfortunately is all that most people at home think of when we mention Saudi Arabia. In the village of Rijal Alma'a, in the Tihama region of Asir Province, we experienced Saudi hospitality first-hand.

We were admiring the 500-year-old stone houses clinging to the hillside when a Saudi resident of the village, Eissa, approached us and enquired if he could be of assistance. I explained that my parents were visiting from the U.S and that we found the architecture of his town unique and interesting. He explained that the region is famous for its painted houses, and asked if we would like to see some of the artwork. I had read about the painted houses of Asir, but I never dreamed that we would be able to see them personally.

Eissa took us to his house, where we had the

honour of meeting his grandmother, Fatima, the matriarch of the family, who is the last remaining woman in the town who knows the art of painting the ethnic designs on the interior walls. She showed us the handmade brushes and paints that she uses in her work, and explained that every design had its own name and meaning. Unfortunately, Fatima who is now over 90 years old, told us that she planned to stop painting.

Because Eissa hopes to preserve as much of the village's unique heritage as possible, he has opened an impressive ethnographic museum in one of the town's old houses. The five- story museum contains exhibits of everyday life–cooking utensils, furniture, tools, jewelry, clothing, weapons, flora, and fauna of the region. The people of the town donated the items on display, and it was wonderful to see the collective sense of pride in their own culture.

After visiting the museum, Eissa took us on a walking tour through the old town, many of its spectacularly painted stone houses now uninhabited and slowly falling into ruin. He reminisced about his childhood days in the village, and showed us the building that used to be his family's house, and another which was the school. We felt very privileged to have been allowed to share in his personal memories and to have caught a glimpse of a unique heritage which is slowly disappearing to modernization and decay.

At the end of the day when we said good-bye, Eissa invited us to stay the night with his family. Unfortunately we had to return to Abha, but not before Eissa made us promise that we would visit again.

 Brad Davis is an American. He is a Logistician and Database Manager at the Royal Saudi Land Forces, Riyadh and has been living in the Kingdom for six and a half years.

My Hometown — Dhahran, Saudi Arabia

By: Steven W. Bisel

In 1947, my father joined Aramco and travelled half way around the globe from San Francisco, California, to Dhahran, Saudi Arabia. World War II had ended two years before and travelling off to foreign lands again must have been traumatic for my parents. My mother and I joined him in 1949. I was three years old. Although very young, I can remember first stepping off the aeroplane at Dhahran and getting my first sight of our new home. My younger brother was born in Dhahran a year later, in 1950. For the next 12 years, this was to be my hometown.

I believe that one's hometown is the place where you spend your childhood. The place of fond memories during the formative years of your life. For me, that place is Dhahran, Saudi Arabia. For when I recall my first baseball game or the names of my school teachers, Dhahran is where it was. I have many memories there, not unlike the memories of millions of others around the world of their hometowns but, there is something very unique about growing up as an expatriate in a foreign land.

I had the opportunity of experiencing two very distinct cultures in my childhood. One was distinctly American, though I was transplanted 12,000 miles from my birthplace. The other was distinctly Saudi. These two cultures were poles apart, separated by language, religion, dress, customs, and history. In the early 50's, it would have been difficult to position two such distinctly different cultures in one place. I truly believe that I have been blessed to be able to experience growing up in Saudi Arabia.

My father's first job with Aramco was as an electrician working on large, heavy duty electric motors. Part of his assignment was to teach Saudi employees the basics of electricity and electric motor operations and repair. He soon became fluent in Arabic and considered many Saudis his friends. Through his relationships, the rest of our family became acquainted and friendly with Saudis. We visited some in their homes, and, although restricted, some visited us in ours. I learned some Arabic and, at an early age, I was exposed to a culture and religion different from mine.

When I was about seven years old, King Abdul Aziz visited Dhahran. There was quite an entourage accompanying him, and I was very impressed. We were let out of school that day to see him. My father was with me. All us children lined up to receive a small tin of English chocolates from the King. He handed me the tin and shook my hand. I thought that was pretty special. Dad told me how the King would allow his people to come and discuss their problems at his palace. He told me that this was the first King of Saudi Arabia and it was he who had united the land. I felt really special to have been able to shake the hand of the first King of Arabia. The chocolate is long gone, but I still have that tin. It is one of my small treasures.

Once, we borrowed one of Aramco's Dodge Power Wagons and went touring for a weekend. We visited the small communities of Dammam, Hofuf, Qatif,

Riyadh, and other exotic sounding places. We saw an old Portuguese fort on the coast and my brother and I played among the ruins. We shopped at Al-Khobar, always a fun experience for us.

"I believe that one's hometown is the place where you spend your childhood".

We also visited some desperately poor communities. I remember how alarmed I was seeing those people and their squalid living conditions—old men with severe disfigurements; people blinded by disease; raw sewage in the streets. These were terrible scenes for a young American kid. The year was 1953 or 1954. I share this experience only because I was able to see these places some five years later. In that short time, roads were built, hospitals, schools, and new homes were constructed. The Saudis were afforded medical care and education. There was considerable change and I understood that oil was the economic force behind these improvements.

I also understood, that although a monarchy, the Kingdom was truly using this new wealth constructively. Here is the first King of Arabia, a man who could easily have taken the vast wealth of the nation and used it purely for his own personal gain, yet he understood that his true and primary responsibility was to help his people.

All of us have witnessed many new emerging nations' leaders ignoring the plights of the people. I truly admire King Abdul Aziz, for wisely using the wealth of the land to lift the tribes of Arabia from virtual obscurity to international prominence. To do so, and to retain the culture and heritage of a proud people, is a grand accomplishment. King Abdul Aziz stepped up to the responsibility to help his people and that is an example that I have tried to live up to, although on a much smaller scale.

Our family spent eight years in Dhahran and four in Abqaiq. It has been a long time since I left Saudi Arabia, but when people ask me where my hometown is, I think first of Dhahran. It may seem strange to some, but not to me. As time passed, I lost contact with most of my childhood friends. My parents are now dead but my brother and I still fondly remember our hometown.

"All us children lined up to receive a small tin of English chocolates from the King. He handed me the tin and shook my hand. I thought that was pretty special".

That period of time in my life exposed me to a land and a people very different to my birthplace. A land that was barren, yet beautiful, with people that were different in language, religion, culture, and habits of dress. I came to learn that these differences were but superficial. I was very young and I could not articulate the reasons, but in the innocence of my youth were planted the seeds of understanding and tolerance that has stayed with me all my life.

I am thankful for those early years of my life when I was given the opportunity of living in a country where I could experience the cultures of two very different societies. I came away with the understanding that we are all one people on this earth. I have tried to share this knowledge with my own children and I am proud to say that I believe I have succeeded.

 Former Aramco employee

As I Contemplate

BY: CHRISTINE BAUMANN

y mother, brother and I joined our dad, Bert Baumann, in Dhahran, Saudi Arabia in September 1963. At that time, I was four years old. My last trip to the Kingdom was as a returning university student in December 1981. Thus, Saudi Arabia was the only home I knew as a child and as a consequence, its culture, climate, history and rulers had a profound impact on me, which remains even to this day.

Let me share one example. I am a transplant nurse who has worked for 11 years in several major transplant centres in the United States. Since these transplant centres are internationally famous, people from throughout the world come to them in the hope of finding a life-saving kidney, liver, heart, pancreas, or lung transplant.

From time to time, these patients are from the Middle East, including Saudi Arabia.

They are frightened at being in a strange country and especially at the thought of facing a very serious operation. Words cannot really describe the expressions of delight and surprise when an American nurse enters their hospital room and greets them in Arabic! More times than not, they notice my name in Arabic on my necklace and ring. While they are patients, I try to make their stay more comfortable by using as much of my sparse Arabic as possible. I still need to use my fingers to count to 10, but I can do it and it always elicits a laugh from the patient.

Perhaps the most important thing is that the patients are relieved at having found a friend who understands something about their home country and culture. Of course, had I not had the privilege of living in Saudi Arabia as a youth, they might never have found a "friend" during their very stressful and lonely stay at a hospital in a foreign country. I've been happy that in some small way, I have been able to repay the hospitality and courtesy shown me by the Saudis

when I was a guest in their country.

My father used to tell my brother, Jeff, and me bedtime stories at night, most of which were fairy tales. However, he felt we should have a sense of the history of the country in which we were guests. Dad would occasionally tell the story of the late King Abdul Aziz and his raid on Al- Masmak Fort in Riyadh, together with his cousin, Abdullah Bin Jiluwi and a band of their followers. In my mind, this was another story he would tell at night, like Robin Hood, and it was just that in my childish mind—a story.
It became real to me one weekend afternoon when

"The simple and dignified life of the Saudi people is something I often think about as I go through the hurried and often complicated life in my own country."

my Dad was invited by our local government relations representative in Abqaiq to attend the opening of a trade school in Hofuf and have dinner that evening with His Majesty, King Faisal. Of course, he told us about the evening and his meeting King Faisal, and I found it hard to believe that this was the son of the man in the story, the future king who drove the forces of Bin Rashid out of Riyadh. The story was really true! Soon thereafter, we took a trip to Riyadh where I saw for myself the Al-Masmak Fort, and the tip of the spear thrown by Abdul Aziz buried in the door.

My childhood years in Saudi Arabia were happy ones. The simple and dignified life of the Saudi people is something I often think about as I go through the hurried and often complicated life in my own country. I would not trade my experiences there for anything and am grateful to the farsighted leadership of Saudi Arabia in establishing the oil industry and making it all possible.

 Former Aramco employee

A Legacy of Vision

BY: ROLF A. CHRISTOPHERSEN

ho would think, in 1951, that a young Saudi like Rauf would rise to lead one of Aramco's largest departments–Office Services.

My friends and I used to play everywhere in Dhahran back then. With a school schedule that let us out of class for one month after each trimester, even though parents and community leaders worked hard to give us wonderful recreation, many of us used to play around the shops area, in the jabal (Hill) to the north by the stabilizer, and in the office areas. We were welcomed wherever we went because the camp was small and intimate, although vigorous.

A portable building to the south of the Administration building's east wing was our joint. The bubbler in Office Services was cold enough to give you a headache. I honestly cannot remember Rauf but I can recall his presence. The portable had several rooms and there were a few desks and chairs in each. Rauf was usually at the desk in the back room when he was not leading the labourers through their tasks of supporting the Administration's dynamic growth and shuffling of office space. From these meagre beginnings, Rauf was to rise to manager of over three million square feet of office space in all Aramco districts, 1,500 employees, and a large budget, by the 1980's. Along the way he received his degree and married the first Saudi to attend the Dhahran Senior Staff School.

Spring ahead in 1982. I am flying back to Dhahran for the first time in 25 years. I have accepted an offer from Aramco to be a Planning and Programs Analyst with Office Services. Thanks to Aramco boyhood friends Steve Furman and Marshall Jones who put my name forward. Rauf is my new boss.

He was not your average department head. He directed his staff from their workspace; he was usually out of his office, either going up the chain to converse with executive management or he was down with us, directing the day-to-day planning. We controlled office space as far away as Jeddah, not to mention Dhahran, Abqaiq, Ras Tanura; frankly, anywhere the company needed office space to support petroleum extraction and delivery. It was so refreshing to work with him, being able to ask questions which required his decision and which he could evaluate and responded to immediately.

I came to admire Rauf's selfless style. Success had not fattened him. He dressed simply in dark slacks and white shirt, well shined shoes, hair trimmed short, and not an ounce of extra weight. His most distinguishing characteristic was his piercing eyes. He was always weighing, listening, directing. He was also very serious, not a backslapper who carried on; he took his work and the company's goals in all sincerity. He was usually the last to leave at night.

Since the 1950s, when he started Office Services, Rauf knew every inch of the company and every policy constructed to cope with the politics and dynamics of office space. I never worked harder since, but my three years with Aramco were wonderful years in terms of accomplishment. I owe that feeling of fulfillment to Rauf. He was a strong leader who knew his job better than anyone else I worked for during my tenure with Aramco.

Strange how our paths diverge and cross. I am a better person for having known and worked with Rauf. Although we were never friends, we were always friendly. I think Rauf is a role model that every Saudi can use as a guide to professional development. His personal methods of approaching a multinational workforce were even-handed and fair. His work ethic was realistic and dynamic.

One has only to visit the Dhahran administrative metroplex to see Rauf's legacy of the early 1980s. He built it and over 8,000 office workers enjoy his vision.

 Former Aramco employee

UNFORGETTABLE MEMORIES

BY: LINDA J. THOMAS

I came to the Kingdom of Saudi Arabia in June of 1989 with an open mind, an open heart and raring for an experience in a foreign land. Everything wasn't perfect, of course nothing ever is, but overall those first memories are treasures. I was lucky enough to have a friend, a nurse colleague who had been here for four years and loved it, and she had given me introductory letters to friends she had who were still in the Kingdom. This allowed me to meet some really wonderful people and my first year here was great. Responsibilities back in America however required that I end my contract after only one year, but I definitely was not ready to leave for good. Three years later, in June 1992, I was able to return.

I dearly love geography and one year after returning I was able to persuade a friend to accompany me on an adventurous journey through parts of the Kingdom. We took the train to Hofuf and Dammam where we explored the cities of Dhahran and Al-Khobar. We took a tour of the caves, enjoyed the corniche by the Eastern sea, and even visited a camel *souq* (market).

We then traveled north by public bus to A'ra'r and across towards the west to Tabuk, near the Jordanian border. We were surprised to find our bus equipped with such modern facilities that included even a video. We passed miles of shimmering desert that seemed endless, varied and awesome, and I enjoyed every minute of seeing this truly magnificent geographical creation. The people everywhere were very kind although they appeared to wonder about our presence, and it was evident that some of them had never seen people from the Western world. We were very discreet of course to respect the cultural beliefs. After six days, tired and weary we took a flight back to Riyadh with many unforgettable memories that will be treasured forever.

My current work involves giving Hyperbaric Oxygen Therapy Treatments, a fairly new field of

medicine, which administers 100 percent oxygen under pressure in a specially designed chamber.

When I came to work in this field of medicine, the Hyperbaric Chamber here at the King Faisal Specialist Hospital & Research Center was the only one in the Kingdom open to the Saudi public. Since then, over the past three years, I have watched with interest the Kingdom's progress in this truly wonderful field of medicine–the Multi-Place Chamber in Al-Jubail has been refurbished and reopened, a Mono–Place Chamber has been placed in a hospital in Buraidah, Qasim, and also Najran, and there are plans to open a large Multi–Place Chamber in Jeddah.

We treat Saudi patients who come from many areas of the country and often these treatments are given daily for three weeks, each one requiring approximately two and a half hours. Spending this much time with a person has given me the special opportunity of getting to know quite a few Saudis personally. I have found them to be very kind, co-operative, and trusting and I consider it a great pleasure

and honour to be able to make a small contribution to their health and well-being.

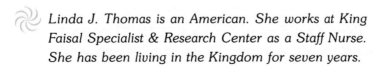 *Linda J. Thomas is an American. She works at King
Faisal Specialist & Research Center as a Staff Nurse.
She has been living in the Kingdom for seven years.*

CLOSE TO UTOPIA

BY: A. M. IQBAL

topia, the word conjures up many possibilities of leading a perfect life and our endeavours to attain that goal. Back in 1976 as a surgeon working in southern India, I was accepted to the post of consultant surgeon for a newly born hospital in the Kingdom of Saudi Arabia. My reservations towards journeying through uncharted waters were numerous as the culture, customs and manners of the people were relatively unknown. But the prospect of adapting to such a unique situation was tantalisingly challenging.

And so I took a decision, which has paid the richest of dividends than all the money in the world.

I have been a resident of this country for 21 years. I have had the opportunity to see this blessed land prosper from an oil producing nation to a vibrant advanced one . Growth in housing, education and public amenities has steadily progressed. Advances in the field of medicine, through better facilities and technological know-how have raised the standards of medical care. The pace at which the health sector is catching up with the developed world is remarkable.

Gone are the days of vast stretches of barren land; in turn replaced by architectural wonders, industries operating on the latest technological wizardry, and the people enjoying a quality of life close to an Utopian reality. The progress of this country bears testimony to the untiring efforts and strong commitment of the house of Saud.

Because of the nature of my profession, I have had the closest of contact with people from all sections of the Saudi community. I have found that the undoubted belief and the faith of the people in the religion of Islam, endowing them with a strong will and character, makes each per-

son special in his own right. The inherent strict morality prevents them from succumbing to frail human deeds and emotions.

As a doctor, I have treated two generations of Saudi families, and my rewards have been the gratification and love that I have received in return. The kindness and magnanimity of a few of my patients have given new lives to orphaned children. Charitable endowments have helped the poor, destitute and the disabled in India. In all my travels, I have rarely come across a nation so peaceful, safe for its subjects, and bringing tranquillity to the soul through the religious laws that govern it.

 A. M. Iqbal is an Indian. He is a Consultant General Surgeon at Riyadh National Hospital and has been in the Kingdom for 21 years.

A Friendship Is Born

BY: GRAHAM SIMPSON

I was sitting in the car. The traffic light was red. I was not looking in the rear view mirror, as I do now. I was looking through the screen into the undeveloped distance. There was a gas station on the far corner with pink fluorescent strip lamps arranged in a saw teeth pattern across the fascia. There was a car waiting to my left, and another to my right but farther away. All of a sudden I heard the wind moving strongly around my car.

It was an impact that moved my car physically to the left. A white flash passed by the right side of the car and visually transformed itself into a car speeding into the distance. What had happened? Was this some kind of desert mirage? There was more to come, the car to my left surged forward and accelerated into the distance, followed by the car to my right.

I opened the door and walked around to the back of the car and then further around to the offside. I looked at the wheel that was only just attached to the axle. The tire was flat. Somehow the chassis was less damaged than I had imagined, though there was an indentation along the entire side. The wing mirror had come off detached and was on the road, somewhere ahead.

> "It was an impact that moved my car physically to the left. A white flash passed by the right side of the car and visually transformed itself into a car speeding into the distance."

It was a Thursday afternoon, the beginning of the weekend, and just after the *Asr* prayer time. It was a long way back to town. There was only the sound of the wind. I wondered how this situation was going to be resolved.

As though in answer a car pulled up behind me and the window slid down. "Can I do anything to help?", a voice enquired. "I don't think so," I replied, thinking only of the damage. I was still trying to comprehend the severity of the situation. "What happened?", the voice continued. It was then that I stopped thinking about the impact and realised that someone was talking to me, helpfully. By then he was out of his car. He wore a brown *thoub* (gown) with which his red and white *ghutra* (head-gear) contrasted. I told him about the collision, the speeding car running a red light and trying unsuccessfully to squeeze between two stationery cars parked at the lights. His name was Ahmed Al- Zahrani, a local businessman in Riyadh.

Some minutes later, the car that had been to my left reappeared and the occupant, an off-duty policeman, informed us that the driver of the car that struck me had been apprehended. A traffic police car appeared and everybody engaged in an animated conversation that my beginner's Arabic couldn't comprehend. The traffic policeman asked a few questions, made some notes, informed me of the accident procedures, and then, positioning his car behind mine, pushed my car through the traffic lights and on to a nearby service road. The swift efficiency with which traffic problems are resolved in the Kingdom has never ceased to impress me.

Ahmed offered to take me home, even though it was in the opposite direction to which he had been travelling. It was the middle of nowhere, or as close to it as you get when you have a car with a wheel missing. It was an offer I couldn't refuse.

When we arrived at my home, I invited Ahmed in and he accepted my invitation. We sat down. We drank tea with lemon, and he smoked. I told him about my family and he told me about his family. We exchanged stories about ourselves, our businesses and our interests.

When Ahmed left, I was no longer thinking about the destroyed car. I was thinking about his thoughtfulness, his helpfulness, his consideration and his generosity. Ahmed had rescued me from a disaster, and given me my first glimpse of an enduring tradition that remains strong in the modern setting of the Kingdom.

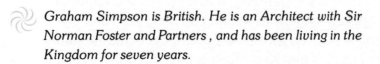 *Graham Simpson is British. He is an Architect with Sir Norman Foster and Partners , and has been living in the Kingdom for seven years.*

I Followed The Footprints

BY: BRUCE HOSKINSON

 came to Riyadh from Florence, where I had spent three years teaching English and completing a degree in Italian. Whenever I think back to my first days of working in the Kingdom, I smile a bit. My first job in Riyadh was as a "decision tracker" on the Peace Sun Program, and my task was to keep track of pending decisions that could hold up progress on a construction program to accommodate 60 new F-15 aeroplanes the Kingdom had just purchased.

When the Saudi buyer in our office came by to order business cards for us, he asked me what a "decision-tracker" did. I explained that I followed the trail of decision-making on the major construction issues and entered this data into a computer to compile a list of the decisions still pending, and highlight the name of individuals or agencies holding up progress. After giving me a puzzled look, the Saudi buyer said he had never heard of that kind of job before, but not to worry, he said, he would obtain an appropriate translation for my card. Several weeks later when he gave me my first business card, it read "decision tracker" in English, and in Arabic as a "follower-of-footprints". I told him that that was an excellent and accurate way of describing my job.

In 1983 I accepted a position with McDonnell Douglas Services as a staff assistant, where I still work today (though it's now called Boeing due to the recent merger). My recollection of Riyadh in that period is of frenetic, all-night construction sites studded with dozens of building cranes, never-ending street detours, and many wrecked or burned-out Toyotas that were actually used as reference points on hand-drawn maps. Looking around at the infrastructure today, I can see that Saudi Arabia has come a very long way in a very short time.

My most vivid and pleasant memories of Riyadh in the 80's are of tennis. Every fall many of us eagerly looked forward to "The Riyadh Desert Classic Tennis Tournament", and in the spring to the annual tennis tournament. As people working in the Kingdom have more quality time available than their counterparts in the States, we expatriates experienced what was almost a second childhood. Every afternoon after work we would get together for hours of tennis. On weekends there was the Riyadh Team Tennis League, which had just started then and fielded six teams in six divisions of different levels of play. Each weekend our team played a team from a different compound. Like the other teams, our team was made up of different nationalities, and I think that the broadening experience of associating with them in work and in leisure is one of the major benefits I gained from living in Saudi Arabia. This was an advantage that still prevails as the many people I met through tennis in Riyadh have remained good friends. I have been lucky enough to visit many of them even after they departed Saudi Arabia. Dick and Inge Morton in Rio de Janeiro, Mario Pepe in Buenos Aires, and Ronnie Gunnarsson in Varberg, Sweden, among others.

There's a common saying that a person learns more about his home country, while abroad than at home because when he sees something new he compares it

with something similar in his country. A side-benefit I've experienced here in Saudi Arabia is witnessing the success (and failure) of products and services of different national origins as they compete in the rich Saudi marketplace. Saudi Arabia has provided me with a free education in international economies and marketing, and I think I've learned more in Saudi Arabia about the strengths and weakness of American products than I ever would have in the States; I've witnessed first-hand the importance of copyrights on intellectual property such as movies, music and computer software, areas in which the U.S. is a world leader.

"There's a common saying that a person learns more about his home country while abroad..."

Perhaps it's because we Americans are not overly tradition-minded, and have a business environment that prizes venture capitalism and fosters creativity, that small companies such as Microsoft, Intel and America Online can thrive and become global leaders. And I've seen, here too, in Saudi Arabia how abysmally weak we Americans are in improving an existing product through continual refinements, which the Japanese refer to as "Kaizen," a technique at which they still excel. I still remember how embarrassed I was several years ago when I saw on the streets of Riyadh one of the ugliest cars ever made—an American gas guzzler—and I remember thinking how much it resembled a whale on wheels. It certainly does not surprise me that Toyota owns half of the vehicular market in the Kingdom.

I've worked in Riyadh now for 17 years, and the fact that I still continue to work here today, when I could work almost anywhere else in the world, implies that I still think this is the best place to be and I see no reason to be anywhere else.

 Bruce Hoskinson is an American. He is Senior Staff Assistant with Boeing-McDonnell Douglas and has been living in the Kingdom for 17 years.

BROAST STARTED IT ALL

BY: DENIS KEARNEY

I came to Saudi Arabia in 1993 having been a teacher in Botswana in Southern Africa for three years before that. In some ways Botswana, a huge country the size of France, could be said to have one thing in common with Saudi Arabia–the massive Kalahari Desert, a very urbanized population and a system whereby the Government looks after the welfare of its population rather well.

However, whereas diamonds are the backbone of the Botswana Economy, Saudi Arabia is synonymous with oil the black gold. That very image conjured up images of petrodollars, sand, sunshine, and of course Islam.

Yet, arriving in sunny Saudi Arabia did bring with it a culture shock. I arrived via my native Ireland and the contrast with green rainy Ireland was blatant from the start. The absence of dark gray clouds, the rain itself and the cool climate was replaced with sunshine, clear skies and a brown sandy terrain.

The existence of so many nationalities particularly in the urban areas was something that led me think Saudi Arabia must be one of the most cosmopolitan countries on earth.

Another contrast I found with Ireland was the newness of the well laid out cities. The roads were superb and the roofs of houses flat as they didn't have to be built to throw off rain or snow. The number of white painted buildings and the sheer massiveness of the houses was something I found very conspicuous.

I gazed in awe at the various building sites where houses were being constructed and marvelled at their sheer size. The amount of marble finishing on the outside of the houses and buildings also came as a surprise.

Of course there was a culture I had to forget once I came to Saudi Arabia the culture of going to

cinemas and theaters. As a measure of compensation for that I was not long in Jeddah when another expatriate friend invited me to go to the beach on the Red Sea. The beach with its smooth crystal sands beside a turquoise blue sea, ironically called the Red Sea– was a haven of relaxation. I soon realized why the beaches of Saudi Arabia are so popular with expatriates.

The sight of broast chicken on almost all the street corners were from the very beginning a mouth-watering experience. I had never seen such an amount of cooked chicken on display as in Saudi Arabia. Chicken, however, I found, only marginally edged out the appeal of mutton and *kabsa* for display.

I have been at a number of Saudi Arabian get-togethers or parties and the sight of huge dishes of rice edged with delicious, soft-cooked mutton and a sheep's head buried in the middle of the rice is for me one of the great delights of Saudi Arabian cooking. It contrasts rather well with Irish stew or Irish beef and cabbage.

Saudi Arabia's relative absence of frost during winter was also a pleasant surprise. Another pleasant but not totally expected surprise was the absence of a society that revolved around drinking alcohol.

Islam and Saudi Arabia are ubiquitous. The presence of so many mosques and of people prepared to close their business and pray in such an organized way was something that impressed me more than anything else.

Despite a number of restrictions I have found life to be quite pleasant in many ways in Saudi Arabia. Apart from the weather and relatively crime-free society, there is the hospitality of the people. Finally there is the opportunity to save money and not withstanding, the other features of Saudi Arabia, like so many other expatriates this is basically the main reason for which I came here.

 Denis Kearney is an Irish national. He is a teacher at the Manarat Secondary School, Jeddah and has been in the Kingdom for five years.

MISSING RIYADH

BY: SANDRA HAWLEY

*L*ooking through the *Nursing Times* (an English Nursing magazine) many years back in Britain, I came across this advertisement for nurses in Riyadh. Interesting. Where was this? Looking up the name in the atlas, I found it was the capital of a country called Saudi Arabia. Instantly images of Lawrence of Arabia and Aladdin came to mind. I applied for a position and to my surprise was accepted. Arriving at Heathrow I met up with three other people who had also been accepted. I tingled with anticipation and a little bit of apprehension. What was I doing?

We arrived in Riyadh just before midnight and cleared Customs in the early hours. As I walked down the steps of the airport, the heat hit me like an oven door opening. We drove to the female nurses' compound, which was opposite the hospital I was to work in. On the door to my allocated villa was a welcome note and inside in the kitchen a very welcome package of groceries and a note from my roommates. Creeping upstairs I found my room and fell into a deep sleep.

I settled quickly into the daily routine. It was a hotch-potch unit of medical and surgical patients with either neurological, ophthalmologic, gastrologic or nephrologic problems. Although I enjoyed my time there I wanted to return to my first love and speciality nephrology, nursing and dialysis. Within one year I was transferred to the renal unit where I had the privilege of working with an excellent team of nephrologists and nurses: Dr Bunono who returned to the Phillipines, Dr Ginn who returned to the States, Dr Quinibi and Dr Furahya who are still employed there (and in my opinion are great doctors) and the nurses, Kathy, Carol, Sylvia, Yvonne and Elise.

Initially I was the only British nurse in the unit. Most of the others were Americans. I had thought we all spoke English, but I quickly found out this was not the case. While working in the isolation room I recall the following exchange between an American colleague and myself:

"Would you get me a flannel please?"
"No problem," came the reply.
First a towel was brought, then a sheet.
"No, I want a flannel," I insisted.
"Look, the only flannel I know is men's flannel trousers," my colleague replied, somewhat bemused.
"No, it's used to wash things."
Her face cleared, "Oh, you mean a wash-cloth."
With that I finally got my flannel.

> *"When it rains in winter in Riyadh get into a four-wheel drive and go out into the desert."*

From then on I developed a keen interest in the correct English of other countries and the difference in meaning to someone from U.K As more British nurses arrived I would sometimes act as an English-to-English translator for them and sometimes for Americans and Saudis who could not understand some British local accents. Very often an American nurse would say something and the English nurse would be very embarrassed, for instance when Carol said... well, that's another story.

The hospital grew in size and advanced in medical technology. As new specialties were added the renal unit became bigger and was moved into a lovely and bright new area. I was privileged to meet many lovely Saudi people from all places and all strata of society.

While the hospital was growing so was Riyadh. When I first arrived in Riyadh, Euromarche was the end of the bus-route. There were four supermarkets and no shopping malls. This changed rapidly. Euromarche became the middle of the town and the Al- Karara Mall opened. What a great place to shop!

While in Jeddah I have heard people say that they prefer Jeddah to Riyadh, but they cannot have seen the beauty of this city. It is not the beauty of Paris

or London, but it is unique in its own right. When it rains in winter (and yes, Riyadh does get rain and it can also be very cold) get into a four-wheel drive and go out into the desert. Mind you don't get caught in a flash flood. Can you see the waterfalls roaring down the escarpment? Turn again and see the desert in bloom, with tiny blue flowers. Turn again and walk over the surface of the moon. Turn again and see the shooting stars. If you want to be energetic, how about hunting for desert diamonds?

During my time at the King Faisal Specialist Hospital and Research Center, I was involved in dialysing various VIP's as well as ordinary citizens, and was privileged to be involved with the first renal transplants carried out in the country. If you ever get the chance to visit the hospital, go to the lobby where a large picture of King Faisal is set into the wall. This picture is a mosaic made of semi-precious stones. I looked at this everyday and gained inspiration.

Why did I leave? Good question. I met my beloved husband and his job was in Jeddah for 10 years. Will I go back to Riyadh? I have been to visit, but I doubt if

I will live there again; yet I will always have fond memories of Riyadh and still have many good friends there.

Sandra Hawley is from the U.K, and has been in the Kingdom for eighteen years.

An Excursion Into The Desert

BY: JOY MAY HILDEN

Our group in five four-wheel-drive cars careened across the desert, satisfied after having a picnic and viewing the fossils in a cave which we had come to see. Now we were hoping to find some Bedouins to visit, so that I could ask some questions and observe techniques of spinning and weaving, if I was lucky. As we dropped from a rise, we saw a line of several tents, and the cars slowly approached, each stopping to visit a different tent. Later we learned that the tents belonged to members of the Al-Murah tribe, the "nomads of the nomads", tough and able to survive the most harsh weather, terrain and living conditions.

Our car, the last, stopped at the smallest tent. There was no movement outside any of the tents; people were resting after the Friday prayers and the midday meal. My friend Pat and I slowly approached the little tent.

Halfway there, a small woman came out, approached and beckoned for us to come and greeted us with a hand shake. Her hand was strong and weathered and she emanated energy and humour. Pat and I communicated in halting Arabic and entered her one room tent. When we couldn't understand her Arabic, she pantomimed expertly.

Soon we were surrounded with children, and later, their mothers, all of them chiming in to the conversation and helping with communication. Our hostess, who appeared to be the aunt and grandmother of the others, served us sweet tea and bitter coffee in tiny cups, along with camel's milk and dates. Mothers nursed their babies. A shy girl, who seemed about seven- years-old, wore a *bookhnoog* , a thin head veil for girls which is decorated with gold embroidery and sewed together under the chin.

The older woman asked about our husbands in the car, and went out to invite them in. They were happy to be included, although it was hard for them to stoop under the low tent opening and to sit on a mat on the ground. I explained my quest, and they seemed impressed that I knew about their weaving and did research in it.

Our hostess wore a black cotton dress that had

"My friend Pat and I slowly approached the little tent. Halfway there, a small woman came out, approached and beckoned for us to come and greeted us with a hand shake. Her hand was strong and weathered and she emanated energy and humour."

been hand sewn and embroidered, a rarity in the days of machine-made synthetics. She said that she had woven her tent, and showed us other things she had made, including a storage bag full of personal belongings, balls of yarn and a spindle. She demonstrated spinning for us, indicating that the camel hair she spun came from the camel herd resting outside the tents. They were in all colours: beige, brown and black, and among them was a new-born.

Our leader came by and said it was time to go. I

bought some yarn and a small weaving used to decorate a camel riding litter, a wooden frame placed on the camel's hump. Thinking that I wouldn't understand, the woman who made it said it was a door ornament. That seemed strange to me, since nomads' tents don't have doors! It was much later that I learned its true use.

Our small group reluctantly said good-bye and promised to return in a couple of weeks. This we did, but that is another story.

ANOTHER WAY OF LIFE

BY: MICHEL SHAWAH

eing in Saudi Arabia is quite an experience indeed. I have been witness to the greatness of spirit and mind of many a Saudi. This is evident in my day-to-day stay in the Saudi capital. Even at work where I am with Saudis, these sterling human qualities are manifested in one way or another. Without this I guess there won't be many expatriates here like me, despite the tax-free, take-home pays.

In my office for instance, I take great delight in the camaraderie I share with my Saudi colleagues. We talk about our lives, we share jokes, and enjoy a brotherly bond that makes working together a pleasant experience. With such harmony it is no wonder that we accomplish much, without noticing time pass by.

Driving from home in Rawdah district to work in the

morning in the Second Industrial Area, some 33 kilometers away, keys me into thinking, and pumps adrenaline into my blood in a manner of speaking. This is how I start my day which goes on to include endless telephone calls and swift moments that go unnoticed until its time to head back to the city centre by evening. My day is usually capped in the night by going out to meet people in Arabian or Lebanese restaurants, either for social or business reasons.

My job entails marketing our products both in the Kingdom as well as in other countries. The GCC (Gulf Corporateion Council) countries have become a big market for us. I keep track of the performance of all the branch managers under me, in different parts of the country such as Jeddah, Dammam, Qassim and others. Over the phone I have managed to develop a close, brotherly relationship with each of them, which has helped us in our common goal of enhancing our company's performance. Sometimes I have to travel to our branches in other parts of the Kingdom, and this gives me the opportunity to see more of the country.

While there is not much scenery to appeal to my aesthetic sense, I feel self-fulfilment in having my innate skills and abilities being put to use. I have become more creative in finding ways to push back any lingering home-sickness and make my stay here enjoyable. My aptitude for sales reinforced by my knowledge of people has enabled me to interact with people meaningfully.

What I especially enjoy is when, on a day off, I have the opportunity to visit places where other expatriates converge. This gives me the chance to unwind and inevitably, slowly, thoughts of home flood my mind. I tend to remember my family and wonder how they are faring. I think about my house and countless other concerns.

During such moments, I run into others who have the same temperament like me. We exchange words, usually, "How are you," and, "How long have you been here?" One good thing about these encounters

is that as you talk you may hit it off, and the day-off paves the way for another new friendship.

What I have discovered is that I can fall back on my ability to adjust and make the culture and environment here part and parcel of my life. It was not easy at first, but gradually I have come to like my life here in the Kingdom.

 Michel Shawah is a Canadian. He works for Plasco for Plastic Industries as a Sales and Marketing Manager, and has been in the Kingdom for two years.

A Kaleidoscope Of Images

James L. Greenberg

1967 : Eight month port delays; unloading cement by helicopters; $150 to sleep on the floor of a hotel; two people sharing the same bed on a shift basis due to lack of housing; hauling water from the city's sweet water plant; airport check in and departures that shared similarities with the start of a camel race; hard, long, often frustrating but innovative exciting pioneering work; buying saddle bags from desert Bedouins; meeting my wife, birth of our daughter (assisted by an Indian mid wife); dare devil sailing on Half Moon Bay; great friends; people of all nationalities with sense of humour and willingness to help regardless of economic station.

1998 : Cities that literally grew out of the desert; whole industries created in a decade; mud and palm thatch houses and packed sand streets become modern buildings, municipal infrastructure, and world class roads; transition from a semi-literate, uneducated population and

small civil service with hand-written records to almost universal literacy and government agencies with growing competence of handling the complex issues facing fast-paced, modern societies; respect for and friendship with many of our Saudi friends and work associates; our children growing up; establishing a solid personal financial base; and a satisfying sense of personal contribution and productivity.

"Cities that literally grew out of the desert...whole industries created in a decade."

These are all part of the "flash images" that make up my personal kaleidoscope of twenty-two years of work, with sixteen years of living experience, in Saudi Arabia. Has it all come together and worked as a well engineered, integrated plan with well-timed execution? Absolutely not. No society and economy in the world has, and most had centuries, not decades to work it out.

As you can probably tell from my kaleidoscope of the "flash images", I have found my experiences in Saudi Arabia personally and professionally rewarding. However, the primarily "hardware" oriented development of the last twenty years, though impressive, has been the easy part.

The next couple of decades must focus on the more difficult "software" aspects of development. Changing expectations of the population within a traditional society; work productivity; modification of the "social-government contract"; economic and social pressures of high population growth; the opening of the economy; and competing in a global market are all issues of staggering proportion. They entail cultural and social changes that take longer than building airports and highways. However, Saudi Arabia has proven itself to be an adaptive and resilient country. These changes will inevitably happen though the specifics of the solutions will take time and will evolve in a Saudi context

 James L. Greenberg is from the U.S. He is Managing Director of the DevCorp International and has been in the Kingdom for sixteen years.

Shocked , Surprised, Amazed

By: Gassim Peer

I have the great honour of being appointed by President Mandela as the first Consul General of South Africa in Jeddah, in April 1996. I took up my post on the first of July, that year.

On arriving in Jeddah my family was greatly shocked by the extreme weather conditions. When we left Johannesburg the previous evening the temperature was minus10C and the next day we performed Umrah in Makkah under a sweltering 48C.

In any event we received a very warm welcome from the Saudi people. I recall that when we moved to our villa, one of our neighbours, Mohammed Al-Ghamdi, invited me for dinner and the entire neighbourhood was also invited to welcome me into the community. We have established a very warm and cordial relationship with our neighbours who have gone to great lengths to assimilate our family into the practice and life style of the Saudis.

I must admit that although my family and I share the religion of the local Saudi people, our customs and traditions are very different and it took us some time to adjust to our new surroundings and appreciate our new found friends and neighbours.

In the past two years, we have really experienced a wonderful life, living and making friends with the Saudi people. Every member of my family has his or her Saudi friend and we share our experiences with delight and sometimes even with amazement.

My children are very fortunate that they have learnt to speak Arabic much quicker that I have, but it was not easy. I recall, how on arrival I had grave reservations when after two months at the Arabic school, my children complained that they could not understand anything their teacher said. However, we persisted and with our support and encouragement my children have now mastered the language. I also recall, with some embarrassment how, on our arrival, when I suffered from a severe tooth-ache my wife took me to a hospital in Madinah to effect an extraction. It was after much debate in sign language that the hospital authorities eventually convinced us that we were in a maternity hospital.

I will be failing in my duty if I did not mention the cordiality and warmth with which all South Africans are welcomed in Saudi Arabia. The Government Departments, Haj authorities, the businessmen and the ordinary Saudis all seem to have a special place in their hearts for South Africa. They are greatly devoted to President Mandela, and in the spirit of their fondness for him they impart to us great kindness which we appreciate very much.

During the 1997 Haj, we had a situation when a young South African boy, suffering from muscular dystrophy was stranded at the King Fahad Hospital, too ill to board a flight home. It was the wish of this young man, who had been seriously ill in South Africa itself, to perform the Haj. The community banded together and along with the assistance of the local Mullah, he duly performed the Haj. He was now too ill to fly back to South Africa.

To transport him home required the payment for and removal of nine seats in the aircraft and the support of a doctor throughout the journey. Help was sought from numerous quarters in South Africa to no avail. However, it took just one appeal from a concerned South African to Prince Majed Bin Abdul Aziz Al Saud, the Governor of Makkah, for His Royal Highness to readily agree to pay for the total cost of the journey. The patient was duly sent to South Africa and a few days after arrival passed away.

"Every member of my family has his or her Saudi friend, and we share our experiences with delight and sometimes even with amazement."

For the 1998 Haj I was surprised to hear that an anonymous Saudi businessman had offered to finance the pilgrimage for 50 needy South Africans.

Through the Saudi Embassy in Pretoria, the persons were notified and to them it was a dream come true. Those I spoke to could not believe that they had been given this opportunity to travel to the Holy Land through the generosity of this individual. They could not find words to express gratitude for the

kindness shown to them. They thanked Allah for His help and requested blessings for the generous donor.

No visitor to the Holy Land can fail to be amazed by the magnificence of the Two Holy Mosques. It took a great amount of vision, courage and dedication on the part of King Fahd, to embark upon and complete these awe-inspiring projects. Pilgrims from every part of the world experience the breathtaking beauty and splendour of the Two Harams and wonder about the foresight and perception of the persons responsible for such a feat.

No expense is spared in ensuring that, despite the arrival of millions of pilgrims annually, the Mosques are immaculately maintained to the highest hygienic standards and to the greatest possible degree of comfort. The sight of thousands of barrels of cold Zamzam water within reach of every person, and the endless supply of disposable cups is alone an achievement to be honoured.

At every level of service one notices the quest for perfect and dedicated service. The authorities have made the decision that the guests of Allah will not be wanting for anything. We pray for their success.

In conclusion I can say that Saudi Arabia is still very much a place of mystery and awe. It is the land of the camel and the desert. It is the land of oil and sand dunes. It is the land of religion and rituals. The land is unique. Its people are unique. Understand their background and many things around you fall into perspective.

 Cassim Peer is from South African. He is the Consul General, South African Embassy and has been living in the Kingdom for two years.

THE KINGDOM GROWS ON YOU

BY: GLENNON J. WILHELM

To be perfectly honest, not many of us would be here if it weren't for the increase in income that is available here and not necessarily elsewhere. That seems to be the primary reason of most people who come here, but once you are here and allow yourself to become part of the atmosphere, the Kingdom grows on you. After some time, you get used to the way of life: slow paced, leisurely, peaceful, with a low cost yet high standard of living.

What intrigues me most about living here is trying to understand the Saudi and Middle Eastern cultures. I have come to realise that the more you think you understand, the less you actually do. That keeps things very interesting and keeps me on my toes!

This is a wonderful place to be, as far as location is concerned, for travel within the country or abroad.

"I have come to realise that the more you think you understand, the less you actually do."

There are many fascinating places to visit in the Kingdom, that are easily accessible. Also, you are within a few hours by air to the entire Middle East and the Asian sub-continent.

I have met many interesting and hospitable Saudis. One time, while we were exploring the desert away from Riyadh, we came across a Bedouin camp occupied by a sheep herder. The Bedouin, invited us into his tent for tea, and offered to slay us a lamb for supper. We stayed on for tea, but could not accept his generous invitation to supper due to prior commitments in the Saudi capital.

We hope to go to the desert again, and I am quite sure that we will come across more Saudis who will show us the same famed Arab hospitality.

 Glennon J. Wilhelm has been living in the Kingdom for seven years. He is from the U.S, and works for Advanced Electronics Company as a Manager of Proposals.

In Riyadh, During The Gulf War

BY: SYED ZEYAD ABU ZAFAR

When I first came to Saudi Arabia in the year 1984 I had conjured in my mind a land of sand dunes, palm-trees and camels, with people in long flowing robes inhabiting it. Imagine my surprise, when I found Jeddah to be a bustling metropolis of marble, with shiny new cars and huge shopping malls! The only things that came close to my preconceived impressions were the palm trees everywhere.

I spent five wonderful years in the city of Jeddah, where I attended the Continental School, before my family moved to Riyadh and I returned to Los Angeles, California.

Coming here from the United States of America, one finds life peaceful, relaxing and secure. The law and order situation in Saudi Arabia, in particular, is something to be appreciated especially by an American.

The cities are clean, well-organised and efficiently governed, I would cite the numerous parks maintained by the local authorities, in such splendor, in the middle of a desert region as prime examples. Prices are cheap, local markets are overflowing with anything you can think of, from apple-pie to zucchini, the malls here would probably put some American malls to shame for their sheer opulence and majestic showcasing of the world's best products.

Along with all this material finery and cultural diversity Saudi Arabia still manages to maintain and enforce moral and ethical practices in life, as guided by the Shari'a laws, in its shining cities and throughout its social structures.

My most memorable memory will always be of the first time I visited the Holy Ka'aba, and the Prophet's (Peace be upon him) Mosque in Madinah. It was inspiring to pray at the magnificent mosque in Makkah which can accommodate nearly a million worshippers. Both the

"We were having dinner with the lights out when an air raid siren started its howling and wailing."

Holy Sites have seen considerable expansion, and their maintenance is exemplary. .

I would be amiss if I did not include my recollections of the Gulf War where Saudi and American forces joined to foil the selfish designs of Saddam Hussein. I was in Riyadh with my father when the war broke out, and the airport was immediately closed. I remember my father coming home with gas masks distributed by his office. We had to tape all the windows in our villa so that the shock-waves from low-flying aircraft and explosions would not shatter them and send glass flying everywhere.

Once, towards the end of the conflict, we were having dinner with the lights out when an air raid siren started its howling and wailing. My father continued to eat calmly, but I jumped up, put on a gas mask and ran up to the roof to see if I could see a Scud missile on its way. At first I could not make out anything but suddenly I heard a whooshing noise, and I saw a long, pencil like object rushing towards a larger, slimmer, pointed missile. I realised I was looking at a Patriot destroying a Scud missile in the sky! With a bang and a puff of smoke, the Iraqi missile had disintegrated in the atmosphere without being allowed to come anywhere near us.

I don't think I felt very scared after that evening on the roof, because as I rushed down to tell my father what I had just seen, a little voice at the back of my mind was telling me that Saddam's Scuds could never hurt my father or me.

 Syed Zeyad Abu Zafar is an American, he is a student and has been in the Kingdom for seven years.

I WOULDN'T HAVE MISSED IT FOR THE WORLD!

BY: NOREEN M. FRETZ

It was March of 1975 and my family and I were in Fez, Morocco, vacationing while on our way to Saudi Arabia to work. Our guide came running from a shop in the *souq* and told us that King Faisal of Saudi Arabia had been assassinated. We were shocked and worried. All of our household goods were already on the high seas headed for Arabia.

What should we do? Do we take a chance and go onwards with our children, Kevin, six, and Jennifer, four?

The U.S Embassy could only tell us that they "thought" everything was quiet. After much agonising, we decided to go.

When we purchased our tickets, we had a choice of connecting cities. We chose Beirut, not knowing too much about Amman or Damascus. Our daughter lost her first tooth on the flight to Lebanon. We were the last passengers to be allowed to enter the terminal.

Thereafter, the planes were refuelled and sent on their way as the civil war was just in the beginning stages.

We arrived at 2.00 a.m. in Dhahran. As we stepped out of the plane the first sight was two parallel rows of soldiers with guns that we had to pass between. It was quite warm and the moon was very bright. I thought to myself, "Oh, boy, what have we done." The terminal was the old one which is now used for visiting dignitaries. It was quite chaotic with people milling around and some assemblage of lines formed that shuffled up to the immigration officials.

We managed to get some of our 13 pieces of luggage and Charlie had the children and myself stay with it out on the sidewalk while he went back to find the rest. There was no one to meet us as we were a day late arriving as one of our flights was late and we missed our connection in Rome. A taxi driver came over and tried taking our luggage. I kept saying no, we're not ready yet. Our cat and miniature poodle were part of our entourage and were in their kennels. This young Saudi taxi driver started to teach my children the Arabic words for cat and dog. I thought ,"This is going to be okay."

This was our first encounter with "Mohammed 44" who drove for Aramco for another twenty-seven years before retiring to his farm in Abha. We returned to Aramco in 1991 after a five year absence and one day, I heard a voice shouting, "Hi, Mrs. Charlie!" It was Mohammed, who still remembered us.

Over the years, we had many wonderful relationships with Saudis. My first houseboy was a kindly man who taught me how to bake date pies and invited us to his son's wedding.

My first boss was Abdul Rahman Dhuahi, probably the most gentle gentleman that I have ever known. I started in Community Services editing movies and videos for Channel Three in 1976. No matter how busy and crazy it got with deadlines always hanging over us, he never raised his voice or made unreasonable demands on anyone.

Over a period of a few years, the editing and broadcasting merged together. We went from editing on equipment that was almost home video quality to state-of-the-art American network standard. At this same time, Aramco was growing tremendously and hundreds of new families were arriving weekly. The Mechanical Services Department commissioned a series of fifty-five training videos to be produced in-house on a variety of subjects.

I was fortunate to be chosen to coordinate the activities of the contracted director and script writers. I travelled the length and breadth of the country by plane, helicopter, and truck as we scouted filming locations–everything from West Pier, the gas plants, to the ARB-1 offshore. It was my job to take still pictures for the "story board" for each video and to keep the crew on budget.

King Khaled did not come to the Eastern Province very often but he did come to inaugurate the opening of the Juaymah Gas Plant. We were there for several days setting up the equipment. The national flag was flying over everything. It was pretty exciting, but the highlight of my time there turned out to be the Rub Al Khali, the vast Empty Quarter of Saudi Arabia.

We had a video to produce on transportation–marine, aviation, and deep-desert convoys. We had been trying to accompany a convoy for several weeks. Finally, at noon one day, we were told to be ready by 6.00 p.m. I raced home to get tents and other camping gear. I was only taking one cameraman and one script writer. The Transportation Department gave us a four-wheel-drive truck with special sand tires. We raced around the Commissary buying food and supplies. When we got to the yard at the Transportation Department, we found out that the convoy had left two hours earlier! We headed south, down the highway and caught up to them where they had just turned off of the road to start heading into the desert. We camped there the first evening.

Each day started before dawn. It was November but the temperatures got well up into the nineties by midday. We would race ahead of the convoy to get set up for taping as they approached us. Many times, trucks would get stuck or tires would blow out. One truck carried nothing but spare tires. Others carried supplies for drilling crews at the end of our trip. Another was a water truck. We had a mechanics truck with all sorts of gear and spare parts. Another carried dinner with live goats and sheep.

"The deeper we got into the desert, the more awesome it became. The dunes were huge and the surface was covered in red sand that had blown in from the Sahara."

The first couple of days were awkward as we were the outsiders and these men had worked together for years. We knew that they would probably invite us to dinner one night and we wanted to reciprocate with something unique.

By our third night out we had plenty of footage so, we invited them to come and watch. We had lugged a big screen TV along. We made popcorn over the campfire and showed our raw footage. They were so excited to see each other on the tape and most had never had popcorn. Later, everyone sat around the fire talking and I just sat back and let the Arabic flow over me. I realized that I understood more than I realized and could actually get the gist of the conversation. Like most fathers anywhere, they talked about their children, the cost of meat from the market, and wanted to be back home with their families. The stars that night were the largest and brightest that I've ever seen. We could see the glow on the horizon of the lights from Abu Dhabi.

When we stopped for tea the next day, a Range Rover suddenly appeared over a dune and a father and son from Abu Dhabi arrived to share our tea break. The father had the most photogenic face and his son was in an immaculate *thobe*. It turned out that he was a finance major at Princeton University in the States.

The deeper we got into the desert, the more awesome it became. The dunes were huge and the surface was covered in red sand that had blown in from the Sahara. The sculpted contours had interesting shadows. With the occasional

flowering bush, it was a photographer's dream. There were tyre tracks leading off in every direction, converging and then separating again. How the convoy leader knew which track to follow was beyond me but he never wavered once.

We arrived at the drilling camp on the sixth day. Even such a small camp seemed busy and noisy after the stillness of the desert. We were given a nice dinner, assigned rooms, and slept in air conditioned comfort. The next morning, we went on an Aramco flight back to Dhahran and culture shock. It took me a few days to adjust back "to the real world."

Often I get bored with being in the States. All of the malls are alike. The grocery stores are boring after shopping in *souqs*. I miss the food vendors and the bakeries. I still have a jar of that red sand on my desk and looking at it reminds me of a magical time in a faraway land.

 Former Aramco employee

LANGUAGE NO BARRIER

BY: TONY GRANT

It's all because I don't speak Arabic. Of course, I know Marhaba (Welcome), Sahh (Right), Shoukran (Thank you) and can breezily assure Mafi Mushkilla (No problem), with the best of them, but that's as far as it goes. Both the following incidents I went through in the Kingdom happened because of defects in my car as well.

The first one happened in the afternoon. I came to my head office, parked the car and went and did my work. When I came out and returned to the car, I discovered I had a flat tyre. It was about five in the afternoon, in July. I was tired and just wanted to get home to a long, cool drink. I went slowly to the boot, opened it, and bent inside to get my spare tyre.

Suddenly, two great big Saudi boys appeared from nowhere. They grabbed me and pushed me forcibly against the wall. I was too astonished to say or do anything. I'd heard of people being mugged, but surely not in Riyadh, and in broad daylight? Having made sure that I could not interrupt their activities, they opened the boot fully, removed my spare and my jack, and proceeded to change my wheel. When they had finished, they put the wheel with the punctured tyre back in the boot, replaced the jack and closed the boot lid. Then they offered me a cold drink, and without waiting for thanks, disappeared with a farewell Ma'salaam.

The second time, it was night and I was returning from Dammam to Riyadh by road. I was nearing Riyadh when for some reason now forgotten, I left the highway and went down the back road that runs around the International Stadium. Here I ran into the National Guard Patrol who were assisting the police in one of their routine checks.

When I say " ran into " I mean that almost literally. I didn't see them in the dark, and had to step on the brakes fiercely. After the check, I tried to start the car, but without success. I know little about cars, but I do know that the battery has two very substantial cables fastened to it. For some reason, there was also a thin cable attached to one of the terminals, and this had parted with the jolt when I applied the brakes.

" Suddenly, two great big Saudi boys appeared from nowhere. They grabbed me and pushed me forcibly against the wall. I was too astonished to say or do anything. I'd heard of people being mugged, but surely not in Riyadh, and in broad daylight? "

I had, of course, no tools, but managed to push the car into the side of the road. I then indicated to the guards that I would leave the car where it was, and walk the rest of the way. Imagine my surprise when I was told in no certain fashion that I was to stay where I was. It was not necessary to know the language to get the gist of what was being said. I did what I was told, but without much understanding. About five minutes later, another car drew up. There was much talk between the Guard and the driver, and before I knew it, I was over and into the passenger's seat.

As the car drove off the driver who, thankfully, spoke English, asked me if I knew what was happening. When I said I didn't he explained that the Guard had instructed him to take me to wherever I wanted to go, as he couldn't have an old man like me walking to the nearest garage.

What I Like About Being Here

By: Aysha Nashwa Ahmed

was five years old when I joined my father, who is working here as an editor for an English daily. In March 1994. My mother Fairooz Nasir Ahmed, works as a Secondary teacher in English, in the International Indian School, Riyadh. I study in the 4th Grade of the same school.

Leaving my grandparents, aunts, uncles and cousins in India was a painful experience for me, but the magic of this wonderful country caught me soon and I forgot all my worries. I am basically a quiet and peace-loving girl and it is this trait of the country and the people here, that attracted me most.

God has bestowed many countries of the world with wealth and prosperity, but it requires a great degree of generosity and tolerance to encompass people of other countries and cultures into one's own country— and that is what the people of Saudi Arabia have achieved.

I am reminded of one particular incident that reflects the magnanimity of Saudis. I go to school in a private taxi, which carries five other students studying in the same school. As usual, we were going to school. The streets were very busy during the peak morning hour when everybody is in a hurry. Our driver had carelessly left the boot of the car in which our school bags were kept, partially open. Half way through our journey one of my friend's bag fell from the boot and its contents were scattered all over the road. Our driver realised the situation but he could not stop the car as it was already far behind, and we could not turn back due to the traffic.

A car driven by a Saudi saw what had happened. The gentleman stopped his car, got out, put the scattered contents of the bag back inside, and raced behind us to return the bag. We had no words to thank him, because many school going cars and buses had passed that way, but none had the consideration to spare their time for strangers. If this kind man had not retrieved the bag, the one-year academic efforts of my friend

would have gone in vain.

I had the opportunity to visit the beautiful city of Al-Khobar, near Dammam, during my last summer vacation. We stayed in my cousin's house in Monopoly Village. Their cottage was charming and cosy. In the evenings we went shopping and in the nights we either relaxed on the beaches or had a swim in the Half Moon Bay. It was one of the most beautiful fortnights of my life.

In Riyadh, we frequently have desert parties which I enjoy. We also visit the lush green, sprawling parks here. When we go to the parks, we usually take our bicycles and have a jolly good ride.

I adore the Kingdom's huge shopping centres and supermarkets. You can get any material thing your heart desires under one roof. The amusement parks and the zoos are other places I love to visit. Recently the Al-Hokair group has started the "Yamamah Resort" where you can swim in simulated "wave pools" and experience the joys of swimming in a real sea.

The unadulterated and tasty food items we get here are another specialty of Saudi Arabia. I specially love the mouth-watering ice creams and chocolates. Saudi Arabia itself manufactures most of the food items we get here, but some items are imported from other countries to suit the palates and tastes of the expatriates living here.

I have been to the Holy Cities of Makkah and Madina which attract millions of pilgrims to the Kingdom every year. The comforts and convenience provided in these two cities by the government for the pilgrims from all parts of the world is truly remarkable.

I am also impressed that the Kingdom provides free education to children of other countries. Our International Indian School itself is a symbol of this generosity. We have been given a license to conduct classes up to Grade 12. As a token of respect to this country, we learn Arabic and Saudi history and culture as special subjects. Thus the Indian students get to know the rich cultural heritage of Saudi Arabia.

If I were to go on writing about what I like about being here, the list would be endless. Hence I'm stopping. I love everything about this country and I wish I could live here for many more years.

I always pray to Allah, the Almighty to bless this country and its people with more happiness and prosperity.

 Aysha Nashwa Ahmed is from India. She is a student and has been living in the Knigdom for four years.

Jeddah Perspective Of A "New Boy"

By: Rod Pemberton

My story begins on a cold, wet day in September or October of 1996.

"This is interesting" she said (she being my wife Sandy).

"What?"

"Jeddah."

"Jeddah?"

"Jeddah."

"O.K. What about Jeddah?"

"A job."

Of course, I had been expecting something like this since we started receiving glowing reports of "expat" life from our eldest boy Richard, who two years previously had gone off to work in Brunei, from which time the first muted mutterings of our never having done anything started.

"Jeddah isn't in Brunei," I said confidently.

"I know." she said "It's in Saudi Arabia, it's by the Red Sea near Makkah."

Knowing that Sandy thought Geography was the

study of rocks, my suspicion was aroused.

"How do you know that?" I asked.

Like magic a copy of the Berlitz travel guide to Saudi Arabia appeared before her.

"Where did that come from?"

"Smiths."

"How long have you known about this?"

"Oh a couple of days, I've phoned for an application form."

"But…"

"It does no harm to look into it."

"But…"

"The boys are grown."

"But…"

"The house is paid for."

"But…"

"It's time we had an adventure."

"But…"

"WHAT!?"

"But I have a job, and a dog and a garden, and re-sponsibilities". I said doggedly.

"Oh and what responsibility might those be?"

Having managed to avoid responsibility for most of my life, I found myself grasping at straws, anything to help maintain my status quo.

"Who's going to walk the dog?"
"Nick."
"Who's going to take care of the garden?"
"Nick."
"And who is going to tinker and mess about with things in the garage on Sundays?"

Of course it was hopeless and even as I said it the reasons for staying seemed like a pretty good argument for going. Forms came and went, interviews came and went, the "well done, your..." letter came, and so did dread. After all those years of stability and routine, we were on the move and not just a little move either. This was a step into the dark, a leap into the void kind of a move, the "I'm making a terrible mistake" kind of a move. That's why on January 18,1997, terminal 4 Heathrow airport, the final frontier, takeoff time fast approaching, I was well into my cups.

The announcement came as a shock even to my dulled senses.
"There will be a two hour delay to the 3:00 p.m. flight to Jeddah, while maintenance work is carried out on one of the engines".

"I wonder if its too late to go by boat" I said.

"I'm going to look round the duty free shops" she said.

"O.K." I said "Waiter, another very large beverage if you please".

After all those years of stability and routine, we were on the move and not just a little move either. This was a step into the dark, a leap into the void kind of a move."

By the time we cleared immigration and baggage check, it must have been going on for 3 a.m. local time, and I must admit to being a little apprehensive, as we were some three hours behind schedule, as to whether or not our contact would still be waiting. It was with great relief that above the general hubbub of the arrival gate I heard my name being called. The drive to our new home from airport consisted of the usual small stock–to be honest I can't remember much of it, by this time. I was suffering from nicotine and caffeine withdrawal (British Airways being a non smoking airline) not to mention fatigue from a journey which had begun at 7:00 a.m. the previous morning, so it was with some relief that we eventually arrived home.

The first thing we noticed about Jeddah was how big things are here: big cars travel along big roads, in our accommodation there is a big cooker with a even bigger oven, kind of a like a Tardis, we also have a big refrigerator, so big in fact that on the hottest days of summer, we hold small tea parties in it, and last but definitely not the least the bed which is about the same size as a small Welsh village, plus if you're into boats, there are plenty of big boats in the local marinas situated on the coast line of the magnificent Red Sea. On visiting the Red Sea for the first time, the first thing you notice is Blue, second thing is Warm, and that it is inhabited by many and varied brightly coloured creatures.

Once past the snorkellers you will see that the fish aren't bad either (Snorkelling tip for you first timers: when trying to attract someone's attention to something interesting-POINT, DON'T SHOUT!)

On reflection my fears and doubts about moving here were founded on the unknown. As the wise man said, Jeddah is what you make of it, and in terms of recreational activities there is something to suit all tastes. Of course there are things that Britain has that Saudi Arabia doesn't: - gales and snow, drizzle, fog, black ice and taxes but I don't miss any of those, and really, the people here are so nice.

 Rod Pemberton is British working for Arabian Homes and has been living in the Kingdom for two years.

WE'RE COUSINS, YOU AND I

BY: CRAIG A. ILGENFRITZ

"**a** balance must be found between the scientific and the spiritual," said the Saudi sitting next to me on the plane heading for Jeddah in early May 1998.

I was going to Saudi Arabia on a study visit by way of a Malone Fellowship awarded to me by the National Council on U.S. - Arab Relations. I did not know my travelling companion, but as soon as the plane was in flight, he began to talk with me and to go out of his way to make me feel comfortable.

"In my country," he continued, "there are those who carry religion to the one extreme, while in the West there are those who only believe in science and technology. To not find balance between the two will end in disaster."

I immediately realized that even though I had not yet set foot on Saudi Arabian soil, I had already encountered, albeit at the individual level, an indication of a fault line in Saudi Arabian society, say, the tension between modernizing social change and tradition.

As I looked around on the plane, I noticed several young Saudi Arabians returning from the United States. None of them would necessarily appear to be Saudi Arabians in the eyes of most Westerners. One young man wore a sharp, pin-striped black suit; another wore jeans and a stylish T-shirt his long black hair hanging down to the middle of his back. A young woman wore jeans and a T-shirt similar to the young man's. Her hair hung loosely over her shoulders.

" His kindness, openness, and invitations said more to me about the well-known phenomenon of Arab hospitality than academic explanations offer. "

"They want to take all of the wrong things from the United States," my companion commented, "MTV and a life of leisure. They want to consume, not to learn the necessary skills for building an economy."

My thoughts went to the expatriates I had seen working for Saudi Arabian Airlines. The expatriate community is 27 percent of the total population in Saudi Arabia by one estimate. As a labour strategy this community is now to give way to Saudisation, a government policy for increasing the number of Saudi Arabians in the work force and replacing the expatriates. The young Saudi Arabian couple with their baby in the rear of our section of the plane also entered my mind. What did being a member of a population that is said to be growing at a rate of 3.2 percent annually mean for that child's generation? To what extent would that child's generation benefit from the current Saudi Arabian modernization project? Would population growth force greater reliance on the traditional structures of the society?

My fellow traveller's comments must reflect such concerns, I was thinking as he exhorted me not to "think of Saudi Arabia as a place where change is not occurring."

"We get information and television from many different places," he went on. "There are many ideas floating around and this cannot be stopped. But we need balance so that change does not become something we do not want. Your country should also take that into consideration."

By the time we were over Egypt, we had discussed the Arab-Israeli conflict, our families, and where we were from. I was even told about my companion's love for honey and its health virtues. He invited me to his home and to a wedding, saying "you must come"; he also invited me to go with him to spend time with the Bedouin in the desert, "this is how I relax when I am not working," he said. I accepted.

As our plane descended to land in Jeddah, I saw many satellite dishes on the rooftops. I thought about the flow of ideas into and in Saudi Arabia, I thought about the future of the country's people, I thought about my companion's concern for balance. I realized that I had experienced an interaction with an individual who mediated a larger picture of Saudi Arabian society for me and stimulated my thinking. More importantly, our conversation underscored our common human interests. His kindness, openness, and invitations said more to me about the well-known phenomenon of Arab hospitality than academic explanations offer. His hospitality spoke to me as an expression of what it means to be human, as the way humans should treat one another, as a way to dispose of the image of the "other".

When I left him to board my flight for Riyadh I said, "You know, we're all related."

"Yes," he replied, "you and I, we're cousins. Call me."

A MEETING OF MODERNISM WITH THE OLD

BY: ERICA SHENTON

Saudi Arabia in my mind is one of the best examples where modern meets old. Despite all the tall state-of-the-art buildings and modern amenities of life that have characterised today's Saudi life, there is much in the Saudi landscapes that is old, such as the mud houses.

When I go to Dirriyah, or old Riyadh, I virtually go back in time admiring the traditional architecture of the buildings and houses. Even here, I can see traces of modernism such as the use of mechanical implements by the farmers. This graphically shows the meeting of modernism with the old.

When I go to a Wadi (Desert valley) I practically relive the past, the silent ambience is indeed reminiscent of the ancient past. Here my parents and I can schedule our activities because my father is in business and can therefore control his work hours. I enjoy the leisurely life during siesta hour, and the complete lack of the hustle-bustle of daily life that is evident in both developed and developing countries.

It takes just a few days stay in my native land, Britain, to make me miss the Kingdom. If I were to leave I would probably remember this country with great fondness.

Erica Shenton is from Britain, she is a student and has been living in

MODERNITY WITH MORALITY

BY: WILLIAM J SOLEY

Looking back, as we sometimes tend to do, I find it difficult to believe that this is the same Saudi Arabia that I arrived at sixteen years ago in 1982, at the "old airport", a very small terminal with little visible technology to support the entry and re-entry systems. I was amazed at the simplicity of life in this vast country.

I remember my first challenge, that of managing a small group of dry cleaners in Riyadh, based in the Mausalat area on the then edge of the desert. The highways were non-existent or under construction; traffic signals, I think there were two sets in the city; petrol stations, the same number. All water was delivered in bowsers, and waste taken away the same way. Power blackouts were frequent, and numerous "no power - no water" situations were almost a daily event.

I remember that if I required clothes and certain medicines or prescription optics I had to bring them back from my next visit to the United Kingdom or go without these.

The life, however, was thoroughly enjoyable and challenging with this certain simplicity, linked with an urgency to expand. Efforts were on to modernise and effect the current stage of the then five-year plan. The city was extremely small but buildings were taking shape in every corner. Roads and hospitals were being built; new shopping malls were under construction; and new services and products kept arriving at regular intervals.

During those early years, the city ended at the lower end of Sitteen Street; the Dammam bridge did not exist; and Talateen Street was then just being built, as was the first Al Akariah.

Those years of development were exciting for all nationals and non-nationals as they represented a future and the change from old to new. It was then that I had the privilege of visiting most of the cities and towns in Saudi Arabia including many of the settlements deep inside the desert. Those experiences are something that I will never forget.

I suppose that originating from the Western world we are largely used to the modern way of life, with all its trappings both good and bad. However, the simplicity of the way of life in Saudi Arabia has made my stay over the years here so enjoyable. I have experienced the more mellow and far less tense way of life, while still achieving my goals.

I have met so many lovely people here who want their

country to go forward while taking care to still hold on to the strong moral values of yesteryear. Indeed this they have achieved in the majority of instances.

Way back in 1982 we would make trips to Half Moon Bay, along a dual carriage way, arriving at a virgin beach with not even a water stop. We now go on a motor way, and the beach is a modern playground for families to enjoy, with every single facility available.

Some years past my wife and I visited the Al-Khaleej

village for a vacation. We would not have found a better spot anywhere else in the world.

We now do not even know where the city ends, enjoy one of the best airports in the modern world, superb hotels and holiday resorts, first class shopping malls, modern hospitals and clinics, advanced telephone links to the rest of the world, and many more modern day facilities, whilst still holding on to the values of moral discipline.

 William J Soley is from Britin. He is a Senior Manager in Saudi American Bank and has been living in the Kingdom for 16 years.

254

HIGH NOTES FROM THE PIANO CIRCLE

BY: GREGORY A. FISHER

 have had 26 years of experience in piano service, research and technology. My training includes factory training at the Steinway and Sons factory in New York, Bosendorfer Pianos in Vienna, and Piano Disk Music Systems Research in Sacramento, California. I also went through specialised training and individual instruction with master craftsmen in the piano industry.

In the Kingdom, I am able to pursue excellence in my chosen profession with continual training and studies for which I have ample time to devote.

Saudi Arabia has always been full of rich and rewarding experiences for me. I recall going to an Embassy that required my services, and upon returning home, I realized with dismay that I had left all my tools in my taxi which had already left. Anywhere else in the world I am sure I would have had to accept the loss of years worth of specialized tools, many of these being one of a kind items, which could never be replaced.

I reported the unfortunate loss to the police. Within a few short days I was amazed to recover all my tools, with not a single item missing. I cannot give enough praise to the efficiency of the police. Of all the places I have travelled I have never known a safer, more peaceful, family oriented society.

One may ask, "What is a highly qualified concert piano technician doing in Riyadh, Saudi Arabia?" I consider it an honour that my respected position takes me into the homes of the finest, most respected and educated families in the Kingdom. The welcome and warm reception I receive here are beyond words. The Saudi families I know are all well educated and kind. Many are fluent in several languages.

To witness first hand such a rapid development in a country is a rarity. Everyday a new project is started, and more are completed not only by the government, but by thriving businesses as well. Recruitment of personnel from around the world also brings its other rewards–the mixture of cultures offers all of us living in the Kingdom the opportunity to share the best food there is to offer, by a host of nationalities.

"Evil is not acceptable in the Kingdom and is dealt with fairly and swiftly "

If you love the different kinds of food around the world as much as I do, well, this is the place for you! (My wife may say the same for shopping!) Local food is inexpensive and plentiful. Nothing can beat the experience of a full moon evening, with fresh fish from the Red Sea cooking over an open fire, beside the smiling faces and laughter of local residents.

If you happen to have even a remote interest in architecture, well your eyes are in for a feast in the Kingdom. With such a mixture of old and new designs, you can feast your eyes on the most amazing buildings imaginable.

To discover the spectacular underwater wonders of
the Red Sea in Jeddah, I took to scuba diving. On
one such occasion my diving partner, a Saudi phy-
sician, after only a few short minutes fifteen meters
underwater, developed a malfunction in his equipment causing him to lose all of his air-supply. I swiftly
responded to this potentially life threatening situation and brought him safely to the surface. His first
words were, "I owe you my life", to which my response was instinctively the most widely used phrase
in the Kingdom- Insha'allah - "It was God's will".

When I am in the U.S many people, for whatever reason, ask me about "terrorists". I simply ask for a local American newspaper, and point out the day's report of innumerable criminal activity. Evil is not acceptable in the Kingdom and is dealt with fairly and swiftly. On the other hand, those promoting peace, doing good deeds, or providing assistance to their fellow men are recognised, rewarded, and received with warmth in Saudi Arabia. I have been to Tabuk, Khamis Mushayt, Al-Khobar, Jubail and many more cities in Saudi Arabia, and never witnessed anything but a friendly, warm and happy people.

I am especially thankful for the time I have for my family, personal development, and creative thought, and a safe and rewarding place to live in harmony with a kind and gentle culture.

 Gregory A. Fisher is a Concert Piano Technician from the U.S, and has been living in the Kingdom for eight years.

SAYING IT AS IT IS

BY: HORACE CAVINESS

Although I adjust fairly quickly, I still experienced quite a cultural shock when my wife and I arrived in Riyadh six years ago.

We had lived in the same house in Dallas, Texas, U.S. for 26 years and had visited only two countries (Canada and Mexico) prior to coming to Saudi Arabia. My first reaction was of fascination as I revelld in observing this entirely new culture.

I discovered that, although our cultures are quite different, there were many similarities. For instance, whether we are Saudis or expatriates, all of us are working for a living, trying to do our best, loving our families, and looking forward to our next vacation.

" To witness people stopping whatever they are doing and praying toward Makkah five times every day, has made a tremendous impact on us "

As an expatriate, the two strongest and most lasting impressions of Saudi Arabia are the hospitality and good humour of its people, and the impact that Islam has on their lives.

The gracious hospitality and generosity of our Saudi friends and acquaintances was and continues to be very impressive. However, even total strangers offer a place around

a meal if our paths happen to cross
at mealtime. From a simple sharing of tea or cardamom coffee to
sumptuous banquets and hours of
their time, I find the people of
Saudi Arabia very generous and
friendly.

I have enjoyed sharing with my
Saudi co-workers the joking and
laughter that helps each of us en-
dure the stress and work of each

day. Each time I hear the words "We have a saying in Saudi Arabia....", I know I am going to be treated with a quotation that is either funny or profound.

My favourite occurred as one of my Saudi friends and I were beginning a journey to the town of Thaddiq in his Nissan pickup truck. The fuel gauge showed that the tank was only half full. I expressed the concern that we may need to stop and buy more petrol and asked if there was a petrol station between Riyadh and Thaddiq.

I have been most impressed with the dedication of the people to their religion. To witness people stopping whatever they are doing and praying toward Makkah five times every day, has made a tremendous impact on us.

What I am impressed with the most is the sight of entire families stopping along the side of the highway, miles from any city and praying. The impression this must have on the children, as they see their parents prostrating themselves before God, will ensure that this religion will continue, generation after generation.

My wife Kathy and I will be making our final exit from here this year to join our two adult children, Kacy and Coy back home in America. We will carry with us fond memories of Saudi Arabia.

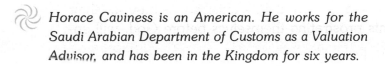

Horace Caviness is an American. He works for the Saudi Arabian Department of Customs as a Valuation Advisor, and has been in the Kingdom for six years.

A Gracious And Generous Society

James Henry Dobson

For most of the ten years my family and I have lived in the Kingdom of Saudi Arabia, first in Riyadh and now in Jeddah, my time has been spent primarily focusing on my professional and family responsibilities. I have managed however, to devote some moments to one of my favourite pastimes, photography.

In the beginning I must admit that the differences between doing business in Saudi Arabia and doing business in my home country, the United States, seemed unending. For instance, I remember being specially impressed to learn that the polite graciousness and generosity fundamental to Arab culture extend into the workplace. Memories of friendly gestures, large and small, decorate my office more beautifully than the most expensive carpets or famous works of art ever could.

Perhaps the most charming and gracious example of Saudi generosity that I have ever observed was through the eyes of a father rather than those of a businessman. Several years ago my wife and I were waiting with our two daughters who were still small at the time, for our flight to leave the Riyadh Airport. A little Saudi girl who was close to my kids in age was also waiting for a flight with her parents. Predictably, the three children were soon together having a great

"Memories of friendly gestures, large and small, decorate my office more beautifully than the most expensive carpets or famous works of art ever could."

from her pocket, put it in my older daughter's hand and then darted off again to join her parents. Such a spontaneous act of giving in one so young was truly beautiful to behold.

Personally speaking, Saudi Arabia has provided me with a unique opportunity to pursue my long-time hobby of photography. In particular, I have enjoyed photographing the desert. Trying to capture its spectacular vistas, stark contrasts and haunting aloneness on film has been an incredibly enjoyable challenge.

I appreciate the graceful way in which life is lived in Saudi Arabia and the country's diverse natural beauty. Inshallah, I hope to continue doing so for a long time to come.

time. The Saudi family's flight was about to leave, so the little girl's mother called for her to come. The girl skipped a few happy steps towards her mother, then stopped, turned around and ran back to my daughters. She pulled a small toy

 James Henry Dobson is the Vice President and Director of Franchise Development at Al-Tazaj Fakieh Bar BQ Chicken. He is an American and has been in the Kingdom for ten years.

Varied Impressions

By: Winifred Anne Ruth O'Allaghan

I have never ceased to be amazed by life here in the Kingdom, especially, in Riyadh, its capital. My impressions are as varied as the people I meet every day.

Riyadh has sometimes been presented in the West as being a "strict city," without character. I do not find it so. Some of the buildings in the city are among the finest that I have seen anywhere, beautifully designed, and reflecting Islamic culture and architecture at its best.

The city is modern, with an excellent modern road network. Too bad that the drivers here do not respect and recognise how lucky they are to drive on such good roads!

As a registered nurse working in the family health

clinics at the King Faisal Hospital, a tertiary care hospital, I find that the service and care given to families and their dependants is second to none. There are many excellent hospitals and health care faculties in the city and improvements are constantly being implemented to improve the lives of the citizens.

Hotels are beautiful, spacious and gracious, and the variety of cuisine and good service to be found is remarkable. This is because there are so many expatriates of different nationalities in the Kingdom to cater to. The shopping complexes are plentiful and varied and most of the boutiques are filled with an amazing array of clothes to suit all the different cultures who live here.

The only Saudi people that I meet are those in the workplace, I find that there is a good interaction between us, with respect on both sides. I am sure that if I spoke more Arabic, the communication would be even better.

I have been invited to a couple of Saudi weddings which were very enjoyable and I find that even though Saudi and Western customs are very different, the warmth and hospitality remain the same. It is a time for getting together with other family members, and close friends for a happy

> "Modernisation of the Kingdom's workforce is occurring at a fast rate. It is marvellous for me as a woman, to see so many Saudi ladies entering the job market."

occasion.

My most memorable experience in Saudi Arabia to date was in Ramadan 1996 when one evening I went out for a walk with 8000 Riyals in my wallet; when I woke up in the morning I found that the money was gone. Despite living in a compound with many people, most of them earning lesser than I do, I was astounded and delighted to discover from the security department that my money had been recovered. Riyal for Riyal. An Egyptian man had found it and handed it over to them. This act greatly restored my faith in humanity.

Modernisation of the Kingdom's workforce is occurring at a fast rate. It is marvellous for me as a woman, to see so many Saudi ladies entering the job market and doing a very commendable job, while still adhering to their strong family values and commitments.

 Winifred Anne Ruth O'Allaghan is Irish. She is a Registered Nurse at King Faisal Specialist Hospital and has been in the Kingdom for two years.

An El Dorado For Architects And Designers

BY: JOHN A. SHENTON

We arrived with some trepidation, expecting a very difficult lifestyle in hot and inhospitable climate and an alien culture, only to find ourselves in a modern and comfortable city amongst friendly and polite people. We decided at first to take an old villa in the suburbs rather than the more expensive option of living in an "expat holiday camp" or compound.

In hindsight it was the best decision we made; my wife as a keen gardener and homemaker quickly transformed a dusty old villa into a real home, we have a lovely pool and a garden to enjoy even on the hottest days and Saudi neighbours whom we count amongst our true friends.

There exists in our street a real sense of community, which bridges any cultural difference. Neighbours smile and greet each other in the street. Coffee invitations are given and accepted. Our children exchange visits and play in each others gardens. I think it is for this more than any other reason that we continue to live in our small villa rather than a super new compound.

> "There exists in our street a real sense of community, which bridges any cultural difference."

I now manage a small but successful Design & Building company, and as an architect I relish the challenge and opportunities of the construction industry here.

As Riyadh continues to grow and flourish towards the Centennial year it is easy to see why it has been such an El Dorado for architects and designers over the past decades. There has always been here a desire for originality and imagination, an expression of the pride in a fast developing nation. Witnesses to this are the many landmark buildings around the city built over the last thirty-five years. The Ministry of the Interior; The Diplomatic Quarter; The Palace of Justice are those that spring immediately to mind, but the list is long.

Today, our clients continue to demand the best in design and finish. Widely travelled, they are exposed to the best of what the world has to offer, and naturally demand the same quality of service and product. Their desire for originality and imagination, however, remains undiminished, and this requires sharp innovation on our part. The increasing sophistication of their expectations together with an acute awareness of value for money means that to survive in this field one has to be wholly professional, and keenly competitive.

This is an environment ripe with the potential to create special works of art–beautiful houses, interiors and gardens, exciting commercial developments and offices, public squares, and parks. The city has many fine examples of these and more on the anvil. Several large and exciting commercial developments currently under construction will give Riyadh world class modern architecture to rank with the finest in any capital city.

Of these the new Saudi Cultural and Heritage Centre is one that will certainly rank among the best museums, with the level of resources being provided for it. The King Faisal Foundation that is currently constructing its New Faisalia Development is bound to astonish. In hot pursuit is Prince Waleed's Kingdom Holding Co. with their magnificent project of similar scale and ambition.

Our office, while not involved in such mega ventures, is kept busy with a multitude of projects that any international architect would be proud of. Just to share in a portion of this enormous potential is reward and reason enough to be here. That my family can lead a comfortable, healthy, safe and enjoyable life is reason to want to stay.

 John A. Shenton is British. He works for Al-Yousef Al-Shaiban Group as an Architect, and has been living in the Kingdom for nine years.

Courageous Decisions Made This Kingdom

By: K.S. Rajan

This part of the world is the most peaceful place today on earth. You only have to work sincerely and efficiently and respect the laws of the country to be a very happy man.

I enjoy going to the deserts and farms. It is remarkable to see hundreds of camels and sheep being driven to the vast open grounds just before dawn and taken back by dusk, all in a disciplined way, controlled by just one individual.

It is an unique feat that such an abundance of vegetable and fruits are grown in the Kingdom's farms, considering the arid conditions. You are totally in a different world here, far from the cities. Sipping Arabic coffee under the aromatic breeze of eucalyptus trees; watching the traditional sword dances; sleeping in motor homes–all these are amazing memories that I will always cherish.

I am a regular snooker player, and am a member of all the major Snooker clubs in town, where most of the players are Saudi nationals. The first Snooker club started in Riyadh about 14 years ago, and today there are more than a dozen Saudi Snooker players of International standard. One of the best clubs in the Middle East is the 'Elite Snooker & Billiards Centre' opened last year in Olaya. Saudi players are very devoted to the game, being co-operative and sporting in spirit. I am sure that in a few years there will be Saudi players among the top ten in the world.

" You are totally in a different world here, far from the cities. Sipping Arabic coffee under the aromatic breeze of eucalyptus trees; watching the traditional sword dances; sleeping in motor homes-all these are amazing memories that I will always cherish."

Some time back, I had both my eyes operated on for an early cataract in the King Khaled Specialist Hospital by a Saudi surgeon, the late Dr.

Ihsan Badr. My family can never forget this part of my life, as it indeed gave me the gift of new light to my almost blind eyes.

At that time I was involved in the mobilisation of a major project at the King Khaled International Airport. While going there one day, I met with a serious accident. My car dashed onto a palm tree on the road near the airport, and I fell unconscious. The airport traffic police on duty found me lying in the almost totally demolished car with my seat belt on. They rushed me to the airport hospital, thereby saving my life. When I regained consciousness I found my family and colleagues near me in the hospital. It was a wonderful job done by the police staff, tracing my employer and informing them of the accident apart from taking me to the hospital in time. I was really moved by this.

With the successful accomplishment of a well-designed five-year development plan that began in

1991, the country has already undergone a physical transformation which most other countries have taken centuries to achieve. Now the Kingdom has reached the sixth development plan which emphasises the need to stimulate the private sector.

On the economic front there has been an impressive growth of Gross Domestic Product as well as in the non-oil sector growth rate. The Kingdom's economy continues to maintain a sustained growth rate despite the unexpected instability in the world oil market. The private sector is responding effectively and the banking sector is doing well.

As a Marketing Manager I have several meetings with officials in the Riyadh Chamber of Commerce. I find that whenever I seek some information the response from the Chamber is something special. They are co-operative, as well as efficient in their service. I am sure they are of great service to businessmen here.

Professor Peter F. Drucker once said that "whenever you see a successful business, someone once made a courageous decision". I feel it is true for a country also–specially the Kingdom of Saudi Arabia. It was initiated by the greatest leader of the country, the late King Abdul Aziz, founder of the unified and modern Saudi Arabia.

 K.S. Rajan is Indian, he works for Saudi Catering & Contracting as a Marketing Manager and has been living in the Kingdom for twenty three years.

NEVER A DULL MOMENT

BY: PERLA S. VEGA

I can never forget that evening in August 1991. When my flight was about to land at the King Khaled International Airport, I couldn't believe that the magnificent site before me, blithe with lustre and discerning of a modern, pompous city, was Riyadh. My bewilderment intensified as I passed through the complex flyovers evident of the wealth of a nation. When I reached the hospital compound where I was to work, I was amazed at the attractiveness of my surroundings, complete with greenery and colourful flowers blossoming all over the place. My housing accommodation itself was almost like that of five-star hotels.

In my first letters home, I described my new surroundings as "almost a paradise, if not a fairy tale". My overwhelming joy was obvious as I described the swimming pools, sauna baths, the gyms and recreational facilities, which were for free use of the employees. When I reported for my duty and met quite a number of colleagues who spoke my native language, I immediately felt at home.

Before I took up employment with the King Faisal Specialist Hospital and Research Center in Riyadh seven years ago, I had misconstrued this country to be venturesome and not right for women to work in. This was even preempted by the idea that living in a foreign country has its misgivings, especially in countries with a complex multi-cultural diversity like the Kingdom of Saudi Arabia. Obviously my first impressions did not last.

Living here has proved to be rewarding not only for monetary compensation but also because of attractive benefits, privileges, safety and convenience. I believe that the longer I stay here the more the place will become like home to me.

What I really appreciate about being here is the peacefulness and orderliness of the surroundings. I can walk around with peace of mind inside or outside my workplace and housing complex. I feel secure wherever I go there are no pickpockets, drunkards, unsavoury characters or violent gangsters to threaten me. The sense of honesty is also impressive. Once I'd dropped my branded sunglasses and thought I'd never see them again, but within no time, and without much ado I was able to retrieve it from the local lost and found department.

In Riyadh, the weather is excellent most days of the year for outdoor sports like tennis. And since recreational facilities are maintained by the employers in impeccable condition as added bonuses to their employees, many expatriate workers become very interested in sports. There are quite a number of tournaments organised, providing respite through friendly competitions as well as the opportunity to make new acquaintances.

The bottom line for me is that life in the Kingdom may be unique, but there is affluence to be enjoyed, and never a dull moment.

 Perla S. Vega is a Filipino. She is a Hospital Assistant at King Faisal Specialist Hospital & Research Center and has been in the Kingdom for seven years.